Reading Matters 1

SECOND EDITION

Reading Matters ❶

An Interactive Approach to Reading

Mary Lee Wholey

Continuing Education Language Institute
Concordia University

▷ For teaching notes, answer key, and other related instructor material, as well as for additional student activities related to this book, go to *college.hmco.com/pic/wholeyone2e.*

▷ To obtain access to the Houghton Mifflin ESL instructor sites, call 1-800-733-1717.

Houghton Mifflin Company
Boston   New York

Publisher: Patricia A. Coryell
Editor in Chief: Suzanne Phelps Weir
Sponsoring Editor: Joann Kozyrev
Senior Development Editor: Kathleen Sands Boehmer
Development Editor: Sharla Zwirek
Editorial Assistant: Evangeline Bermas
Senior Project Editor: Margaret Park Bridges
Associate Manufacturing Buyer: Brian Pieragostini
Executive Marketing Manager: Annamarie Rice
Marketing Associate: Andrew Whitacre

Cover Images: Background photograph: © Photodisc Photography/Veer.com.
Thumbnail photographs from left to right: Noted author Jeanne Wakatsuki Houston reads from one of her works at the Cesar Chavez Public Library in Salinas, CA (AP Photo/The Salinas Californian, Richard Green); 1919 photo of Albert Einstein in his study, age 40 (AP Photo/NY Times); Dalai Lama reads through his speech during a function at Dharamsala, India (AP Photo/Angus McDonald); Young Helen Keller reading a book in Braille © Bettman/CORBIS; Members of the Philadelphia Eagles relax in the stands at Alltel Stadium in Jacksonville, Fla. (AP Photo/Stephan Savoia)

Photo Credits: p. 0: © Digital Vision/Getty Images; p. 1: © Jeff Greenberg/The Image Works; p. 3: © Tom Prettyman/PhotoEdit; p. 12: © David Young-Wolff/PhotoEdit; p. 18: © Ellen Senisi/The Image Works; p. 44: © Michael Newman/PhotoEdit; p. 45: © Ted Spagna/Photo Researchers, Inc.; p. 55: © Spencer Grant/PhotoEdit; p. 58: © Michael Newman/PhotoEdit; p. 80: © Richard Shock/Getty Images; p. 81: © SuperStock, Inc./SuperStock; p. 92: © C. Wilhelm/Photex/zefa/CORBIS; p. 95: © Michael Newman/PhotoEdit; p. 102: © Rhoda Sidney/Picture Person Plus/The Image Works; p. 106: © Nancy Sheehan/PhotoEdit; p. 114: © The National Trust Photolibrary/The Image Works; p. 118: © Frank Pedrick/The Image Works; p. 119: © Michael Steele/Getty Images; p. 120 (top left): © Mike Powell/Getty Images; p. 120 (top right): © Brad Wilson/Getty Images; p. 120 (bottom left): © SuperStock, Inc./SuperStock; p. 120 (bottom right): © Alan Jakubek/CORBIS; p. 132 (left): © Mike Chew/CORBIS; p. 132 (right): © William Bachman/Photo Researchers, Inc.; p. 137 (left): © Anne-Marie Weber/Getty Images; p. 137 (right): © Paul Souders/Stone/Getty Images; p. 144: © Michael Wong/Getty Images; p. 149: © Topham/The Image Works; p. 162: © Stockbyte/SuperStock; p. 163: © Time & Life Pictures/Getty Images; p. 166: © Hank Morgan/Photo Researchers, Inc.; p. 169: © SuperStock, Inc./SuperStock; p. 174: © P.J. Hendrikse, Pietersburg, South Africa; p. 178 (left): © Paul Harris/Getty Images; p. 178 (right): © David Rosenberg/Stone/Getty Images; p. 196: © Rob Lewine/CORBIS; p. 208: © Pete Saloutos/CORBIS; p. 209: © Darren Robb/Stone/Getty Images; p. 220: © B.S.P.I./CORBIS; p. 223: © Walter Hodges/Getty Images; p. 226: © GDT/Getty Images; p. 235: © Owaki-Kulla/CORBIS; p. 249: © Burkina Faso/Panos Pictures; p. 251: © www.spirituallifeinstitute.org

Post-it® Notes is a registered trademark of 3M Company.

Library of Congress Control Number: 2005934052

Student Text
    ISBN-10: 0-618-47512-5
    ISBN-13: 978-0-618-47512-4

Instructor's Examination Copy
    ISBN-10: 0-618-73256-X
    ISBN-13: 978-0-618-73256-2

23456789-CRS-10 09 08 07 06

Contents

Introduction to the Second Edition

The *Reading Matters* series is a four-level reading program comprising texts at the high-beginning/low-intermediate, intermediate, high-intermediate, and advanced levels. It fosters the development of active readers through a multifaceted approach to interaction: interaction with the text, with other readers, and with readings from sources beyond the classroom. This new edition includes new and updated readings as well as additional readings in the "Expanding Your Language" section of each chapter. The *Reading Matters* series features stimulating extensive reading combined with intensive practice provided by well designed tasks that develop both fluency and accuracy at each level. The series incorporates the latest approaches to teaching productive strategies—from understanding the purpose and nature of different texts to guessing meaning from context, learning vocabulary for academic and professional success, and learning how to access information in the media and over the Internet.

In brief the series provides for:

- The development of active readers through interaction with a variety of texts, with other readers through reading-retell tasks, and with authentic reading outside of the classroom.

- Thematic units featuring high-interest, level-appropriate, informative topics that include texts about culture, science, the environment, business, innovation, sports, and entertainment.

- A wide variety of reading types, such as articles, interviews, essays, charts, and graphs.

- A skills and strategies overview of the comprehensive reading skills and strategies in each chapter that feature the development of critical thinking and information processing.

- Opportunities for personal reading, writing, and speaking activities.

- An index of key vocabulary aimed at both academic and professional needs (provided at *college.hmco.com/pic/wholeyone2e*).

- Access to the *Reading Matters* Online Study Center website, which includes individualized learning and testing materials, at *college.hmco.com/pic/wholeyone2e*.

Extensive Reading

To develop fluency in reading, students need significant exposure to text—that is, extensive reading. Extensive reading provides the opportunity to develop automatic text-processing skills. *Reading Matters* offers high-interest reading selections of sufficient length so that readers get the chance to increase the amount of time spent in silent reading. Variety in text styles is an important component of extensive reading. The series features a variety of styles and genres including articles, interviews, graphs, and charts, so that readers develop an awareness of the scope of reading as well as the various purposes for which texts are written. Authentic texts or adapted authentic texts are used at appropriate levels.

Intensive Reading

Reading Matters features thematically-related units on topics of interest and relevancy today. These topics range from social issues, scientific advances, the environment, and the business world to the fields of leisure, entertainment, and culture. The activities in each unit help students develop fluency and accuracy in reading by activating two complementary text processing methods: top-down and bottom-up.

The Process of Reading

Top-Down

Reading Matters enhances the approaches readers use to understand reading globally. In this series, the readers' background knowledge of the topic and critical thinking skills are engaged and readers are encouraged to make predictions about what they expect to find in a text. The reader reads to confirm or modify these predictions and begins to build a mental framework of the information in the reading selection. Awareness of rhetorical patterns, such as chronological ordering, cause and effect relationships, and other discourse features aids in the comprehension of information from the reading. In addition, *Reading Matters* helps the reader develop an awareness of the range of reading strategies, such as skimming, scanning, or previewing, that readers have at their disposal. The ability to apply these strategies appropriately is an important component of reading competency.

Bottom-Up

Knowledge of grammar and vocabulary has an effect on reading ability. Although readers can predict content from their knowledge of text structure or their background knowledge, a certain level of vocabulary recognition is required for processing text. *Reading Matters* introduces and develops vocabulary-building skills through such activities as guessing from context, recognizing meaning, grouping words, and identifying the use of special terms. Well-designed tasks help the reader learn new vocabulary and key words in the text. In the context of thematic units, the reader's vocabulary develops naturally through exposure to a range of texts. Students engage in a gradual process of acquiring key vocabulary by building from a basic level of vocabulary to a wider net of related terms. Students build their understanding through repeated use of language that contains key concepts and information.

In addition to a solid vocabulary, fluent readers have a good knowledge of syntactic structure.

Actively examining the important grammatical features of a text provides a meaningful context for this kind of learning. To build reading competency, the amount of exposure to reading as well as the identification and practice of learning strategies for both vocabulary and grammar are tremendously important. *Reading Matters* provides direction to readers through activities in the "Vocabulary Building," "Expanding Your Language," and "Read On" sections.

Skills Integration and Interaction

Reading is an active process. Interaction between and among students helps to facilitate this process. In exchanging ideas about the information in a text, readers confirm what they have understood. This confirmation process helps to develop accuracy in reading. It also provides a motivation as well as a clear purpose for reading. Interaction with other students can be best accomplished when speaking tasks are an integral part of a reading activity or the activity leads to the undertaking of writing tasks.

The interrelationship of skills integration and interaction requires a holistic approach to task design. The activities in *Reading Matters* are sequenced, and the recycling of tasks in various combinations allows the progressive development of reading competency in ways that are fresh and effective. The tasks are structured so that the learner builds skills and strategies progressively but in ways that offers challenge as well as variety. In *Reading Matters*, the reader uses and reuses the language of the selection both implicitly—to bolster an answer—and explicitly, as in the exchange of information from paired reading selections that provide complementary or contrasting information on a topic. Readers orally explain the information from their reading selection to readers who chose a different selection. Then, together, they apply that information to carry out a new activity.

Text Organization

Reading Matters 1 contains six thematic units with three chapters in each unit. In the second edition, each chapter features one to three reading selections. Many readings have been updated and new readings have been introduced. The unit themes feature topics of high interest to both academically-oriented and general audiences. Most importantly, the selections are of sufficient length for students to progressively develop fluency in reading. Through the chapter readings, students are able to build a rich semantic network without sacrificing variety so that interest in the topic is not exhausted. Within each unit, reading selections are structured so that the information from one selection can be compared with another.

You can choose among the chapters of a unit selectively to suit the needs of various program types and teaching approaches. Complexity in both text type and length, and difficulty in task type are structured to build gradually from chapter to chapter and unit to unit. Some overlap in level of language and task is built into each of the texts in the *Reading Matters* series so that you can accommodate the various levels of students within a class.

Unit Organization

Each unit in *Reading Matters 1* features the following components:

▶ Introducing the Topic: This introductory section identifies the theme. It features the unit opener photo and quote, which are designed to stimulate the readers' curiosity about and prior experience with the theme, or its personal relevance. The tasks are interactive and draw on a variety of media: text, photos, and graphics.

▶ Chapters: The three chapters in each unit present various topics loosely related to the theme.

Chapter Organization

For each of the reading selections the following tasks are presented:

▶ **Chapter Openers** include pre-reading reflection and discussion questions, graphs, questionnaires, surveys, or illustrations. The purpose of this section is to stimulate discussion of key ideas and concepts presented in the reading and to introduce key vocabulary. Encourage students to explain their ideas as completely as possible. Teach students strategies for maximizing their interaction, such as turn taking, eliciting responses from all group members, and naming a group leader and reporter. Whenever possible, re-form groups to give students a chance to talk more until they feel comfortable with the topic. Elicit key ideas and language from the students.

▶ **Exploring and Understanding Reading** contains content questions of varying levels of complexity. These questions guide students in the development of their reading strategies for improving general comprehension, developing an awareness of text structure, and evaluating the content of a text in detail. Emphasize the purpose of the activity and how it is tied to the development of a particular strategy. Point out the ways in which students can apply their skills to reading assignments. Help students build their tolerance for uncertainty. Point out that the purpose of comparing and checking their answers with the information in the reading is to verify as well as to become familiar with the information in the reading. Act as a resource to help students find the accurate information. An answer key that the instructor can use as needed is provided on the *Reading Matters* website at *college.hmco.com/pic/wholeyone2e.*

▶ **Paired Readings** include interactive Recapping, Retelling, Reacting to the Reading, and Discussing the Story activities that involve oral presentation of information from the readings, oral exchanges of information, and discussion that involves critical evaluation of ideas, including comparison/contrast and debate. At this level, talking about the reading they do is crucial for improving students' language use. Emphasize the importance of explaining the information in as natural and conversational a style as possible. Help students to develop their skill at extracting important information from a text by pointing out the purpose of note taking, highlighting, and underlining key information. Emphasize the importance of practicing at home for in-class presentations.

▶ **Vocabulary Building** comprises tasks that introduce vocabulary-building strategies such as the understanding of key terms, the interrelationship of grammatical structure and meaning, using context cues, and developing other aids to the fluent processing of reading selections. This edition adds exercises in each chapter that focus on learning the meaning of verbs and working with word form and function to foster the understanding of academic and general vocabulary.

▶ **Expanding Your Language** presents activities that offer students additional opportunities to use the material and strategies in the chapter. This section often includes additional extended readings. Encourage students to use these activities to further their own comprehension of the readings. Through these activities, students can improve their speaking and writing fluency.

▶ **Read On: Taking It Further** presents opportunities for personal reading and related activities, including suggestions for further reading as well as reading and writing journal entries, keeping a vocabulary log, and word play. Although most of this work will be done outside of class, time can be found in the class schedule to report on some of the activities. This gives students a purpose for the work and practice in developing their reading skills and strategies.

Reading Matters Online Study Center Website

Students gain confidence in their reading abilities as they discover how to access information more easily from the press, over the Internet, and in their professions or fields of study. The Internet activities give students a chance to consolidate and extend their reading skills. Using the *Reading Matters* website offers students the opportunity for productive work on an individual basis at any time of day or night that's convenient for them. Students are directed to the Online Study Center website at the end of each chapter.

Reading Matters Online Teaching Center Website

As with all Houghton Mifflin textbooks, there is a specific website devoted to necessary teaching tools that come in handy while using the text. Instructors using *Reading Matters* can access useful chapter notes and the answer key at the site. In addition, there are downloadable chapter tests that instructors can administer to students. These tests focus on comprehension skills and important vocabulary. Finally, a sample syllabus is included for instructors who need some guidelines about how to use the text effectively throughout the semester. To access the Online Teaching Center, go to *college.hmco.com/pic/wholeyone2e.*

Acknowledgments

I am grateful to Susan Maguire, who first suggested the idea for the series. A special thanks goes to Kathy Sands Boehmer and Sharla Zwirek, who have been an invaluable help throughout the lengthy process of bringing this manuscript into its present form. Thanks also to Margaret Bridges and the rest of the production and editorial staff at Houghton Mifflin.

My gratitude to the people who read the manuscript and offered useful suggestions and critical comments: Jesus Adame, *El Paso Community College;* Fred Allen, *San Jose City College;* Jim Epstein, *University of Arizona;* Melinda Johnson, *Allan Hancock College;* Gary Prostak, *Los Angeles Mission College;* Enid Rosenstiel, *Ohio State University;* and Donna Tooker, *Grossmont College.*

I would like to acknowledge the support and inspiring work of colleagues and students at the Continuing Education Language Institute (CELI) of Concordia University in Montreal. A special thanks goes to Adrianne Sklar for her advice and suggestions after reading drafts of the material. The continuing support of Lili Ullmann, Phyllis Vogel, and Nadia Henein has been invaluable to me. Thank you also to Tanya Ullmann, who helped in the preparation of the answer key, and to Ioana Nicolae for her help in preparing the student website.

Finally, thanks to my family—Jerry, Jonah, and Yael—who haven't given up on me, even though they've heard, "Can't right now, got to finish this work," for years on end.

Mary Lee Wholey

Reading Matters 1: Overview

Unit	Skills	Activities	Vocabulary	Expansion
UNIT 1 **Communication: Talking to Each Other**	• previewing titles (1) • marking questions in the margin (1) • asking questions before reading (2) • using illustrations to retell information (2) • predicting (3)	• getting information from illustrations (1) • matching ideas and details (1) • problem solving (1) • recapping, retelling, and comparing stories (2) • matching pictures and captions (3) • matching questions and answers (3)	• vocabulary in context (1, 2, 3) • categorizing (1, 3) • meaning of verbs (1, 2, 3) • word form (1, 2, 3) • going from general to specific information (2) • prepositions (3)	• answering a questionnaire (1, 2, 3) • answering *wh*-questions (1, 3) • personal writing (1, 2) • role playing (3) • topic writing (3) • extensive reading on the topic (1, 3) • keeping a vocabulary log (3) • studying online (1, 2, 3)
UNIT 2 **The Mysteries of Sleep**	• previewing a reading (4, 6) • reading an advice column (5) • identifying a speaker (6)	• answering a questionnaire (4) • problem solving (4) • recapping, reacting to, and retelling a story (5) • problem solving (5) • getting information from illustrations (6)	• vocabulary in context: nouns and verbs (4, 6), adjectives (5) • jigsaw sentences (4, 5) • categorizing (5) • antonyms (5) • sentences with *but* (5) • meaning of verbs (4, 5, 6) • word form (4, 5, 6) • past tense verbs (6) • word play (6)	• asking questions and giving answers (4) • role playing (5) • two-minute taped talk (5) • discussion questions (6) • topic writing (6) • studying online (4, 5, 6) • keeping a vocabulary log (6) • extensive reading (4, 6) • reading cloze (6)
UNIT 3 **Relationships**	• predicting information (7) • identifying a speaker (7) • understanding the main idea (8) • previewing (9) • finding key words (9)	• categorizing information (7) • getting information from an illustration (8) • completing a chart (8) • recapping, reacting to, and retelling a story (8) • looking for similarities and differences between two stories (8) • agreeing and disagreeing (9) • note taking (9)	• vocabulary in context: (7, 8), nouns and verbs (9) • meaning of verbs (7, 8, 9) • word form (7, 8, 9) • verb /preposition combinations (7) • past tense verbs (7, 9) • categorizing (8) • antonyms (8) • prepositions (9)	• role playing an interview (7) • writing information from an interview (7), graph (8) • role playing a conversation (8) • two-minute taped talk (8) • personal writing (8, 9) • talking about benefits and problems (9) • studying online (7, 8, 9) • keeping a vocabulary log (9) • extensive reading (8, 9) • reading cloze (9)

Unit	Skills	Activities	Vocabulary	Expansion
UNIT 4 **The Challenge of Sports Today**	• reading in groups of words (10) • predicting information (10, 12) • identifying the main ideas of paragraphs (10, 11) • answering content questions (10, 11, 12) • note taking (10) • listing the facts (11) • comparing information from two readings (11) • identifying supporting points and details (12)	• answering information questions (10) • note taking (10) • making a decision (10) • problem solving (10, 12) • getting information from illustrations (10) • recapping, reacting to, and retelling a story (11) • getting information from a chart (12) • using information to complete a chart (12)	• antonyms (10) • word form: noun endings (10) • vocabulary in context: (10), adjectives (11), past and present (12) • guessing meaning from context (10) • jigsaw sentences with *when* (11) • verbs and prepositions (11) • meaning of verbs (10, 11, 12) • word forms (10, 11, 12) • past tense verbs (12) • word play (12)	• making an oral presentation (10) • personal writing (10, 11) • preparing a questionnaire (11) • two-minute taped talk (11) • role playing (12) • topic writing (12) • extensive reading (10, 11, 12) • studying online (10, 11, 12) • reading cloze (12) • keeping a vocabulary log (12)
UNIT 5 **Technology for Today's World**	• previewing (13) • finding advantages and disadvantages (13, 14) • understanding main ideas (14) • locating and highlighting important information (14) • predicting information (15) • understanding examples (15)	• making an argument (13) • finding similarities and differences between stories (13) • getting information from a graph (14) • making a chart to list facts (14) • recapping, reacting to, and retelling a story (14) • matching ideas and examples (15) • problem solving (15)	• vocabulary in context (13), verbs (14), phrasal verbs (15) • linking with *instead of* and *but* (13) • recognizing definitions for technical terms (14) • meaning of verbs (13, 14, 15) • word forms (13, 14, 15) • word play (15)	• asking information questions (13) • two-minute taped talk (14) • topic writing (14, 15) • making a questionnaire (14, 15) • extensive reading (13, 14) • reading cloze (15) • reading the news (15) • studying online (13, 14, 15) • keeping a vocabulary log (15)
UNIT 6 **Leisure**	• using key words to find information (16) • understanding examples (16) • previewing (16, 18) • recognizing advantages and disadvantages (17) • making comparisons within a reading (17, 18) • identifying details (18) • using highlighting to make a list (18)	• giving your opinion (16, 18) • asking questions (16) • getting information from a graph (16, 18) • recapping, reacting to, and retelling a story (17) • listing advantages and disadvantages (17) • identifying the speaker (18)	• vocabulary in context: nouns and verbs (16), (17, 18) • antonyms (16, 17) • categorizing (17) • meaning of verbs (16, 17, 18) • word forms (16, 17, 18) • nouns and verbs (18)	• reviewing a movie (17) • writing advantages and disadvantages (18) • questionnaire (18) • reading cloze (18) • extensive reading (16, 17, 18) • studying online (16, 17, 18) • keeping a vocabulary log (18)

Communication:
Talking to Each Other

When people talk,
listen completely.

—*Ernest Hemingway*

Introducing the Topic

We communicate in many ways. In this unit, we will find out about some common forms of communication. Chapter 1 is about nonverbal communication, or body language. In Chapter 2, we will find out about two interesting cases of multilingual communication. Chapter 3 presents the story of Post-it® Notes, those handy pads of paper that are used for leaving messages everywhere.

▶Points of Interest

What do you think this person is trying to say?

Reading Body Language

▶ Chapter Openers

Discussion Questions

▶ **Communicating Without Words** Think about these questions. Share your ideas with a partner or with a small group.

1. What is body language?
2. How do we learn to use and understand it?
3. Why is it important to understand body language?
4. Is it possible to read body language the wrong way? How does that happen?

Getting Information from Illustrations

▶ **A** For each of these sentences, write its letter on the line under the illustration that matches it best.

> **Reading Tip**

Illustrations can help you understand ideas in the reading. Discussing the pictures gives you a chance to learn useful language. ■

a. Hello!

b. I don't know.

c. Nice to meet you.

d. I'm so happy to see you. It's been so long!

e. Everything is great. OK!

f. I'm really worried.

1. _____   2. _____   3. _____

4. _____   5. _____   6. _____

▶ **B** Look at the illustrations again. Describe how each person is communicating. Name what part(s) of the body that person is using.

1. Would you use the same body language to communicate each message?
2. If not, what body language would you use?

▶ **C** Work with a partner. Take turns talking about each illustration. Say as much as you can.

▶Exploring and Understanding Reading

Previewing

> ➤ **Reading Tip**

The **titles** can contain the important ideas of a reading. ■

▶ **Titles** Look at the titles in the reading. Check (✔) the titles that you find in the following list.

1. _____ Eyes
2. _____ Ears
3. _____ Hands
4. _____ Arms
5. _____ Legs
6. _____ Body
7. _____ Head

▶ Now read the article and learn about some of the ways we use our bodies to communicate.

What Language Does Our Body Speak?

Body language isn't a language of words in English, Spanish, Arabic, or Japanese. It is a language without words. Body language isn't verbal; it's nonverbal. People communicate nonverbally in many ways. It's natural to use our bodies to communicate. Gestures are powerful communicators of our thoughts and emotions. What are some of the important ways people communicate with body language? Is body language the same all over the world, or does it change from one culture to another?

Head

Let's start with the head. Most people around the world nod their heads up and down to mean "yes" or "I agree with you" and side to side to mean "no." These are almost universal signs, but there are a few places where it has the opposite meaning. It is possible that people first communicated with these signs thousands of years ago.

Eyes

Our eyes communicate meaning. But people from different countries communicate differently with their eyes. In the United States, it is important to look into the eyes of the person you are talking to. But if you look for more than a few seconds, people will think that you are staring. Staring is impolite. People will ask themselves, "Why is that person staring at me?" In other countries, such as England or Israel, it is usually polite to look for a longer time at the person you are talking to. It shows you are interested in talking to the person. In Japan it is not polite to make eye contact for long. It is better to lower your eyes when you meet someone.

Hands

We often use our hands to communicate ideas and emotions. In many countries, people greet each other with a handshake. In the United States, the custom is to take the other person's hand and hold it firmly. But in the Middle East, the custom is to take the other person's hand gently. All over the world, people wave their hands to say hello or goodbye. But people wave differently in different countries. In Europe the correct way is to put your palm out and keep your hand straight, moving your fingers up and down. Americans wave with their whole hand.

We can use hand signals to send a short message. But we need to be careful. We don't want to send the wrong message and cause a misunderstanding. In the United States, for example, people make a circle with their thumb and forefinger to say "OK" or "Very good." In France, that hand signal has the opposite meaning. And in South American countries, that signal is an insult! In Japan, it is the symbol for money. In the Middle and Far East, it is impolite to point with the index finger. Showing the "thumbs up" signal is an almost universal sign that means "OK."

The Whole Body

We show emotion nonverbally with our whole body. We open our arms to show welcome or to hug someone. We turn away from someone we disagree with. People tap their feet or their fingers. This shows that they feel angry or impatient. When we feel comfortable, our bodies look relaxed. When we feel uncomfortable, our bodies look tense and nervous. In the United States, people cross their arms in front of their chest when they feel anxious.

In these days of global communication, people do realize that things are done differently in different cultures. So people will understand if you make a mistake and send the wrong signal. The best advice to follow is to watch what people do, and follow what they do. A careful look at how people act will teach you how to communicate. Although body language has a lot to say, it doesn't use words.

Understanding Details

▶ **A** Circle the letter of the correct answer. In the reading, underline the words that support your answer. In the margin of the reading, write the question number.

1. Body language is a
   a. verbal language.
   b. nonverbal language.

2. Most people move their heads ——————— to mean yes.
   a. side to side
   b. up and down

3. In the United States, it is ——————— to look into the eyes of the person you are talking to.
   a. important
   b. not important

4. In the United States, it is ——————— to look at a person for more than a few seconds.
   a. polite
   b. impolite

5. In the Middle East, it is the custom to greet people with a ——————— handshake.
   a. gentle
   b. strong

6. We use hand signals to send a ——————— message.
   a. long
   b. short

7. We open our arms to someone to show that we ——————— them.
   a. welcome
   b. disagree with

8. The meaning of body language is ——————— everywhere.
   a. the same
   b. not the same

▶ **B** Answer the following questions. In the reading, underline the words that support your answer. Write the question number in the margin.

1. What will people in the United States think if you look at someone for more than a few seconds?

   _____

2. What do we use our hands to communicate?

   _____

3. People make a circle with their thumb and forefinger. What does it mean in:

   a. the United States? _____

   b. France? _____

   c. South American countries? _____

   d. Japan? _____

4. How do Americans show that they feel anxious or nervous?

   _____

5. How will people react if you send the wrong signal?

   _____

6. What should you do to learn how to communicate nonverbally in a new culture?

   _____

▶ Work with a partner. Take turns reading the completed answers to each other. Refer to the reading if you have different answers.

Matching

▶ Match the actions with parts of the body.

Parts of the Body	Message/Action
_____ 1. Arms	a. Say "no."
_____ 2. Hands	b. Look at the person you are talking to.
_____ 3. Eyes	c. Say "I agree with you" or "yes."
_____ 4. Head	d. Greet for the first time a person you don't know.
	e. Say "OK" or "That's great."
	f. Say "Goodbye."
	g. Give someone a hug.

▶ Work with a partner. Make a question to ask your partner for information. For example, you can ask your partner, "What kind of message(s) can you give with your eyes?" or "What can you do with your eyes?" Take turns asking and answering questions.

Reacting to the Reading

▶ How do you send these messages nonverbally? Indicate what part(s) of the body you use and how you communicate your message.

Message/Emotion	Part(s) of the Body	How to Communicate
Hello.		
Come here.		
It's good to see you.		
Sorry.		
Call me later.		
I'm angry.		
I'm surprised.		
You're late.		
Watch out.		
Don't come here.		
Come here quickly.		
Are you talking to me?		
I have a headache.		
Bring me the bill.		

▶ Work with a partner or a small group to show how to use body language to send your messages.

Problem Solving

▶ **Applying the Information** Think about the ideas in the chapter reading. What kinds of problems could people in the following situations have?

1. A student from country X is meeting a fellow student from country Y for the first time. Student X puts out his hand to greet student Y. Student Y looks uncomfortable.

2. A student is 20 minutes late for her appointment with her professor. The professor is sitting tensely at her desk and is tapping her pencil on the desktop.

3. You are walking with two classmates. One classmate, a young woman, sees a young man who is a good friend. She hasn't seen him for a long time and gives him a big hug. Your other friend looks away.

4. You are working with a group of people. Someone makes a hand signal that you don't understand to another person.

5. You are talking with a young woman but are not looking directly into her eyes. You are not sure whether she understands you.

▶ **1.** Discuss the situation with a partner. Decide what problems these people could have.

2. Think of some possible actions that would solve the situation so that the people feel comfortable. Try to agree on what you would say or do.

3. Present to the whole class your explanation and solution for each situation.

❯Vocabulary Building

Word Form and Meaning

▶ **A** Match the words in Column A with their meanings in Column B.

Column A	Column B
_____ 1. advise	a. to give a sign
_____ 2. communicate	b. to obey or to copy
_____ 3. differ	c. to be unlike or to have an opposite idea
_____ 4. follow	d. to give information to someone
_____ 5. signal	e. to make a suggestion or offer counsel to someone

▶ **B** Study these five words in their various forms: verb, noun, adjective, and adverb. The forms are not in the same order in each column. Then choose the correct form to fill out the chart below. These words are commonly found in general and academic texts.

advise (v.)	communicate (v.)	differ (v.)	follow (v.)	signal (v.)
advice (n.)	communication	differentiate	following	signaler
advisor (n.)	communicatively	difference	follower	signaling
advisory (adj.)	communicative	differently	following	signal
advisedly (adv.)	communicator	different		

Verb	Noun	Adjective	Adverb
communicate	1. 2.	1.	1.
differ 1.	1.	1.	1.
follow	1. 2.	1.	
signal	1. 2.	1.	

▶ Compare lists with a partner. Try to agree on the same answers.

▶ **C** Write three sentences using words from the list.

▶ **D** Often a word has the same form when it is used as a noun and as a verb. Look at the following sentences and indicate if the word in **boldface** is used as a noun (N) or as a verb (V). Mark *N* or *V* on the line provided.

1. _____ I didn't understand the **signal** to stop talking that she was trying to give.

2. _____ I tried to **signal** to her to save me the seat next to her.

3. _____ Sometimes, the **signals** he sends are hard for me to understand.

4. _____ Be careful not to send the wrong **signals** when you communicate.

5. _____ When the light changes, that's the **signal** you should cross the street.

6. _____ We agreed that she would **signal** to me when she wanted to leave.

Vocabulary in Context

▶ **A** When you don't know the meaning of a word, you can use the words you do know to help you make a good guess. Use your understanding of the words or phrases in **boldface** to help you guess the word that is missing.
 Complete each sentence with one of the following words.

| a. arrive | b. ask | c. complete | d. discover | e. experiment |
| f. increase | g. lose | h. schedule | i. surprise | j. train |

1. I worked at the library **for the first time** and was happy to _____ that I could do all my homework quickly.

2. It will _____ you **to find out** how much more you can do when you study early in the morning.

3. She had many **questions** that she wanted to _____.

4. She had to _____ all the work that was left **before she could go home**.

5. My friend was late and I **waited over an hour** for him to _____ at the library.

6. I'll **check my agenda** to see if we can _____ a time to get together and finish the project.

7. I decided to _____ by **getting up at different times** until I found the best time to study.

8. It takes **time and willpower** to _____ yourself not to answer the phone when it rings.

9. The **answering machine is on** because I don't want to _____ study time talking on the phone.

10. You can _____ your productivity by **getting up fifteen minutes earlier than you normally would every day**.

▶ **B** Work with a partner and take turns reading the completed sentences.

> **Tip**

Refer to the readings to help make your choices in the vocabulary activities. ■

▶ **C** Complete each sentence with one of the nouns from the following list. Use the words in **boldface** to help you choose your answer.

| a. advice | b. countries | c. customs | d. handshake |
| e. head | f. hug |

1. People around the world nod their _____ **up and down to mean "yes" and side to side to mean "no."**

2. And in **South American** _____, that signal is an insult.

3. The best _____ is to watch what other people do **when you're in a situation where you don't know** how to act.

4. People **greet each other** with a _____.

5. In the Middle East, the _____ for greeting people are **different from those in the United States.**

6. She **opened her arms** to give her friend a big _____.

▶ Compare your answers with a partner. Then take turns reading the completed sentences.

▶ **D Categorizing** Circle the word that does not belong in each of the following groups. Prepare to explain the reason for your choice.

1. head   hand   people   fingers
2. North America   South America   Middle East   England
3. signal   message   sign   eyes
4. hug   thumb   tap   wave
5. hello   goodbye   OK   handshake
6. tense   nervous   happy   anxious

▶ **Pair Work** Tell your partner the answer and the reason why it doesn't belong.

▶ Expanding Your Language

Reading

This reading expands on the idea of how we communicate without words. Notice how much easier it is to understand this now that you have already done some reading on this topic.

▶ Before beginning, read the following questions. After reading, answer them based on the information in the text.

1. Who is Paul Ekman?
2. What does he teach his students?
3. What does he show his students?
4. What do they have to identify?
5. Why do we have trouble recognizing people's facial expressions?
6. How long does it take to learn to read people's faces?
7. What kind of people are interested in Paul Ekman's work and why?

Is Your Face an Open Book?

Paul Ekman is one of America's most well-known experts in the area of human personality. In fact, he is a psychology professor at the University of California at San Francisco. Ekman teaches his students how to read faces. To do this he shows his students pictures of human faces. He shows each face for just one-half to two-and-a-half seconds. Then he asks them to identify the emotion that person is feeling. He asks them to say whether the face they see is angry, afraid, surprised, sad, or happy. If you think this is an easy exercise, you are wrong. It's not as easy as you might think to learn how to recognize people's emotions. In fact, in our modern life we learn to hide our emotions and to ignore the signals we get from facial expressions. In one in-class exercise, the students answered only half of the questions correctly. It takes a few hours of study before they learn how to be better "face readers." There are many people who are interested in Ekman's work. People such as film animators, religious leaders, and police officers study with Ekman. Ekman helps them to recognize the emotions that show in people's faces, even emotions that show for as little as one or two seconds. This is information that makes them better at the work they do. In some cases, such as in police work, reading a person's face could even save a life.

Speaking

▶ **Questionnaire** Answer these questions. Be ready to explain your answers. Interview two classmates and ask for their answers to these questions.

1. Is it easy or difficult to understand nonverbal language? Why?
2. Can you use body language to tell people that you agree or disagree with them? How?
3. Can you show people nonverbally that you are happy to see them? How?
4. When you are working in a group, can you signal people that you want to speak? How?
5. Do people from different cultures have different ways of using body language?
6. Is it easy or difficult to learn the nonverbal language of another culture? Why or why not?

▶ **Pair Work** With a new partner, take turns telling the answers you received.

Writing

▶ **Personal Writing** Write six to ten sentences about how you use nonverbal language when you communicate. You can use some of the ideas from this chapter. You can describe some special nonverbal signals you use.
   Follow these steps:

▶ **1.** Think of ideas you want to write about. These ideas could include special body language people use in your country, the way that body language can communicate ideas more easily than words do, or why it is important to "read" body language.

   2. Write a list of all the ideas you want to include. Think of the details or examples you have to explain your ideas.

   3. Use these ideas to guide your writing.

   4. Write your ideas in complete sentences.

Online Study Center For additional activities, go to the *Reading Matters* Online Study Center at *college.hmco.com/pic/wholeyone2e*.

Communication Across Cultures

Chapter Openers

Questionnaire

A When Do You Use English? Answer these questions for yourself. Then ask two other classmates to answer the questions. Put a checkmark (✔) in the appropriate column for each answer.

Questions	Yes	No	Sometimes
1. Do you use English when you			
a. talk to friends?			
b. go shopping for food?			
c. go out to listen to music?			
d. read magazines or newspapers?			
e. go to the movies?			
f. go to a party?			
g. are at home?			
h. go shopping for clothes?			
2. Do you ever speak your native language and English mixed together when you			
a. talk with friends?			
b. talk with family?			
c. talk at work or school?			
d. shop for food or clothes?			

▶ **B** Now answer these questions about celebrations.

1. What are some special celebrations you have during the year?
2. What food do you make for these celebrations?

Celebration	Food
a. Thanksgiving	Turkey and pumpkin pie (United States)
b. Birthday	Cake and ice cream (United States)
c. _____	_____
d. _____	_____
e. _____	_____

⬤Paired Readings

> **Reading Tip**

Asking questions before reading is a good strategy for helping you to understand more about the subject of the reading. Some important question words are *who, what, where, when,* and *how.* ■

▶ In this section, you will find two different stories on the same theme. Choose one of the two to work with. Prepare to explain the story to someone who read the same story and then to a person who read the other story.

▶ These are two stories about the lives of some people who live in the United States but whose first language is not English. One story is about neighbors who live in the same apartment building but speak different languages. The other story is about bilingual people who mix English and Spanish. What questions could you ask about the daily experiences and lifestyles of people who speak languages other than English? Here is an example.

Question: When do people speak their second language?
Answer: When they are at work.
When they are at school.
When they are at the supermarket.

▶ Write three questions of your own.

1. _____

2. _____

3. _____

▶ Choose one of the stories to read. Work with a person who is reading the same story.

❶Sharing Our Worlds

Understanding Details

▷ Read each paragraph and then answer the questions. In the paragraph, underline the words that support your answers.

Twelve Languages in One Apartment Building

❶   Casa Heiwa is the name of an apartment building in downtown Los Angeles. The name comes from the Spanish word "casa," for house, and the Japanese word "heiwa," for harmony, or peace. Casa Heiwa is a special place to live. People who live in this apartment building speak twelve different languages. In the building are signs in five main languages—Japanese, Chinese, Korean, Spanish, and English—for exits and what to do in case of fire. At building meetings, people communicate in six languages because both Mandarin and Cantonese Chinese are used. The other languages people speak are Vietnamese, Indonesian, Laotian, Tagalog, Thai, and Zapotec.

1. What is Casa Heiwa?

   _____

2. Where is it located?

   _____

3. Why is Casa Heiwa special?

   _____

4. What does Casa Heiwa mean in English?

   _____

5. How many languages do people use at building meetings?

_____

❷   People learn from one another about different traditions and different customs. Trying food from other cultures is one of the exciting exchanges that people share. The apartment building managers plan parties for special celebrations at the building. On the Fourth of July, people bring their own traditional food to the apartment party. Korean families bring *kimchi*, and the South American families bring dishes of roasted peppers. On Thanksgiving, the building managers bring a traditional turkey to every family. Each family cooks the turkey in its own way. Families from Central America cook the turkey in orange juice. One Asian family cooks it like a Chinese-style duck. People learn to eat new foods and to enjoy new customs, such as traditional music and dances, that they learn from one another. They gain an awareness of how much they share.

1. What do people learn from one another?

a. _____

b. _____

2. What parties do the managers plan for?

_____

3. What kinds of food do families from different cultures bring on the Fourth of July?

Cultures	Food
_____	_____
_____	_____

4. What do the managers bring on Thanksgiving?

_____

5. What do families from different countries do on Thanksgiving?

_____

❸   Casa Heiwa is an apartment building where people can learn some important life skills and how to cope with living in a new environment. The building managers run a service that offers a number of programs to children and adults. For the children there is a day-care center that operates from 7 A.M. until 6 P.M. This is good for the children and for the parents. The children can learn in the same building they live in while the parents are at work. There are also educational programs available for older children and adults. These programs include computer processing and English reading and conversation courses. They help children get assistance with homework or have a tutor if they need special help. There is also a job-training office in the building where people can come and get career counseling and job placements that will benefit them. Finally, there are programs like Family Movie Night that give everyone a chance to do something together. Casa Heiwa is a special place to live, designed to give people a sense of community and a sense that they belong. Everyone who lives there thinks that Casa Heiwa is a good place to live.

1. What can people who live at Casa Heiwa learn?

   _____

2. What programs do the building managers have for children?

   _____

3. What educational programs are there for older children and adults?

   _____

4. What services can people get at the job-training office?

   _____

5. What programs are there for the whole family?

   _____

6. Why is Casa Heiwa such a special place to live?

   _____

▶ Work with a partner. Take turns reading the questions and answers. Refer to the reading if you have different answers.

Recapping the Story

▶ Reread the first paragraph quickly. Cover the information and tell your partner as much as you can remember. Ask for help if you forget or give incorrect information. Take turns reading and retelling the information in all three paragraphs.

 Retelling Tip

Use the illustrations to help you remember and explain the details of the story. Show your partner the illustration as you are explaining. Explain as much as you can. ▪

Reacting to the Story

▶ Share your ideas about these questions with a partner.

1. Would you like to live in a place like Casa Heiwa, where people speak many different languages and share their different customs? What are the good and bad points of this type of experience?
2. The story names the foods that people from different cultures prepared. What other customs could people learn from one another?
3. The building managers at Casa Heiwa try to offer programs for the people who live there. How do these programs help people feel more a part of the community?

❷Sharing Our Words

Understanding Details

▶ Read each paragraph and then answer the questions. In the paragraph, underline the words that support your answers.

Speaking "Spanglish" in Nueva York

❶   In New York City, two young Hispanic women are talking at lunch. Each woman speaks Spanish perfectly. Each speaks English perfectly. And they both speak Spanglish. Spanglish is a mixture of the two languages. How do people make up words in Spanglish? Take an English word, such as *rave* (an all-night dance and music event popular among young people), and put a Spanish-sounding ending on it. This is called borrowing. Another thing people do is to take an easy word in English, such as *parking*, and use it in a Spanish sentence. This is called switching. People say that Spanglish is easy and that it's fun to speak and to understand if you're bilingual.

---

1. What languages do these women speak?

   a. _____

   b. _____

2. What is Spanglish?

   _____

3. What is borrowing?

   _____

4. What is switching?

   _____

5. What two things do people who speak Spanglish say about their experience?

a. _____

b. _____

❷   Spanglish is very popular in New York City, Miami, and Los Angeles. These cities have large Spanish-speaking populations. In these cities, you can hear Spanglish on the community radio stations. Some young musicians write songs that have Spanglish words. Where can you find written Spanglish? You can find Spanglish in popular magazines, novels, and poetry. People like to use Spanglish for various reasons. One man says that it just sounds better. Another says that sometimes there isn't a word in English or Spanish that expresses the thought he wants to get across. So he uses a Spanglish word. One woman says that when she's speaking English, she sometimes uses a Spanish word because it expresses her feelings better than English does. It's easier to talk about such emotions as joy, anger, or love.

1. Where is Spanglish popular?

_____

2. Where can you hear Spanglish?

_____

3. Where is Spanglish written?

_____

4. What are two reasons people say they use Spanglish?

a. _____

b. _____

5. Which emotions does one woman say are easier to talk about in Spanglish?

_____

❸   Will Spanglish grow? Some people think that it will. One man is writing a Spanglish-English dictionary. Spanglish has a practical use. The fact is that there are some words such as "Kleenex," that people use throughout North and South America that are replacing the Spanish words that people used to use. There is also the increasing effect of the Internet. You can turn on your computer to *surfear* the Web. If you make a mistake and you want to remove it, then you'll have to *deletear* the lines. Technology is one fact of modern life that is changing the Spanish language. For example, when people send e-mails they don't usually have the accents on the words they write. People say that Spanglish helps them to express their identity as both Hispanic and American. It shows that they are comfortable with themselves. It's creative, and it fits their lives today.

1. What is one man doing to increase the use of Spanglish?

_____

2. What does the use of a word such as "Kleenex" show is happening today?

_____

3. What are two Spanglish words that are used because of Internet use? What are their meanings?

   a. _____

   b. _____

4. What is one example of the effect of technology on Spanish?

_____

5. What does the increasing use of Spanglish show?

_____   _____

▶ Work with a partner. Take turns reading the questions and answers. Refer to the reading if you have different answers.

Recapping the Story

▶ Reread the first paragraph quickly. Cover the information and tell your partner as much as you can remember. Use the illustrations to help you. Ask for help if you forget or give incorrect information. Take turns reading and telling the information in all three paragraphs.

Reacting to the Story

Retelling Tip

Use the **illustrations** to help you remember and explain the details of the story. Show your partner the illustration as you are explaining. Explain as much as you can. ■

▶ Discuss these questions with others, and give the reasons for your answers.

1. Do you ever mix the words from two languages or speak both at the same time? Explain when and why.

2. How do you feel when you combine words from two languages when you are talking?

3. How do you think the Internet will affect changes in languages like Spanish?

Comparing the Readings

Discussing the Stories

▶ **A** Work with a partner who read a different story. Tell your partner the details of the story you read. Use the illustrations to help you tell the story. Then listen to your partner's story.

▶ **B** Complete this task with your partner. Circle *T* for true and *F* for false. If the statement is false, give the correct information.

1. T F   People who live at Casa Heiwa speak ten different languages.

2. T F   People all over the world speak Spanglish.

3. T F   At Casa Heiwa, people don't celebrate any holidays together.

4. T F   People use Spanglish when they talk, write, and sing.

5. T F   At Casa Heiwa, the building managers bring people turkey on Christmas.

6. T F   People use Spanglish only when they feel angry.

▶ **C** Circle the statement you think is true for both stories.

1. People can use their first language and their second language together.
2. People cannot keep their own traditions when they live in another country.
3. People can learn new customs and languages, enjoy them, and make them their own.

▶ **D** Discuss the "Reacting to the Story" questions for both stories. Explain your answers as much as possible.

❱Vocabulary Building

Word Form and Meaning

▶ **A** Match the words in Column A with their meanings in Column B.

Column A

_____ 1. assist

_____ 2. express

_____ 3. identify

_____ 4. operate

_____ 5. remove

Column B

a. to recognize what something is

b. to tell something or explain an idea

c. to help someone

d. to run something or make something work

e. to take away something or delete it

▶ **B** Study these five words in their various forms: verb, noun, adjective, and adverb. The forms are not in the same order in each column. Then choose the correct form to fill out the chart below. These words are commonly found in general and academic texts.

assist (v.)	express (v.)	identify (v.)	operate (v.)	remove (v.)
assist (n.)	expression	identifiably	operational	removal
assistance (n.)	expressively	identifying	operation	removable
assistant (n.)	expressive	identification	operating	removed
assisted (adj.)	expressed	identifiable	operationally	
assisting (adj.)		identity	operator	

Verb	Noun	Adjective	Adverb
express	1.	1.	1.
		2.	
identify	1.	1.	1.
	2.	2.	
operate	1.	1.	1.
	2.	2.	
remove	1.	1.	
		2.	

▶ Compare lists with a partner. Try to agree on the same answers.

▶ **C** Write three sentences using words from the list.

▶ **D Adjectives to Nouns** In English, the form of the word can change when it is used as a different part of speech. For example, a suffix (ending) can be added to change the adjective *expressive* to the noun *expressiveness*. Some common noun suffixes include *-ness*, *-ment*, *-ence* or *-ance*, and *-tion*.

Choose the correct form of the word for each of the following sentences. In the parentheses ( ), write the part of speech, noun (N) or adjective (ADJ), needed to complete the sentence.

1. different / differences

   a. The people at Casa Heiwa speak at least twelve _____ ( ) languages among them.

   b. Tenants think that the _____ ( ) among their languages makes it easier for them to use English to communicate.

2. new / newness

   a. They were a little afraid to speak because of the _____ ( ) of talking to so many people.

   b. Living in the apartment building was a completely _____ ( ) experience for her.

3. expressive / expressiveness

   a. She always thought of herself as a very _____ ( ) person and someone who was never shy.

   b. The kind of _____ ( ) she used in her teaching helped her students understand even the most difficult ideas.

4. nervous / nervousness

   a. She kept asking her girlfriend, "Why do I feel so _____ ( )?"

   b. It was difficult to understand the _____ ( ) she felt.

5. aware / awareness

   a. I was surprised by the _____ ( ) of the situation she showed.

   b. They were _____ ( ) of the many different feelings she had.

Vocabulary in Context

In written English, ideas are often presented in an organized way. First, a sentence presents a general idea. Then the next sentence has a specific detail or example. Here is one example of this kind of organization from the story.

People bring their traditional food to the party. Korean families bring *kimchi,*
(general)   (details)

and the South American families bring dishes of roasted peppers.
(details)

▶ **A** Look back at the readings in this chapter and find three more examples of this pattern. Write them on the lines below.

General   **Specific**

1. a. _____   b. _____

2. a. _____   b. _____

3. a. _____   b. _____

▶ **B** Complete each sentence with one of the verbs from the list. Use the words in boldface to help you choose your answer.

a. bring	b. communicate	c. enjoy	d. hear
e. speak	f. understand	g. use	

1. They _____ learning new customs and they **have fun** eating food from different countries.

2. They **talk** in Spanglish to _____ their feelings to one another.

3. In many cities, you can _____ Spanglish **songs on the radio**.

4. I _____ in my first language **when I talk to my family**.

5. To **improve my speaking**, I _____ my second language at home.

6. I asked people to _____ some food for everyone to share **when they come to the party**.

7. I _____ the language because I **learned it in school**.

▶ Compare your answers with a partner. Then read the completed sentences.

C Categorizing Based on the chapter readings and information of your own, complete the following list with words that belong in the categories.

Countries/Regions	Languages Spoken	Traditional Foods
1. United States	English	Turkey on Thanksgiving
2. _____	_____	_____
3. _____	_____	_____
4. _____	_____	_____
5. _____	_____	_____
6. _____	_____	_____

Options Interview your class members and add to this chart with information from the other students. List as many possibilities as you can.

Expanding Your Language

Speaking

A Answer these questions for yourself. Then interview two people in your class. Ask them to answer these questions.

> **Tip**

How to Form a Question
- Begin your question with *Do* or *Did* or use the helping verb in the sentence, as in this example:
Do you like to swim? or
- Use a question word such as *who, what, where, when, why,* or *how,* to begin the question. For example:
What kind of music do you like? or *Where do you go to talk with your friends?*

You

1. What different languages can you speak?
   a.
   b.
   c.

2. What languages do you use
   a. at home?
   b. at school?
   c. at work or school?
   d. with friends?

3. What are your favorite activities in
   a. reading?
   b. listening?
   c. talking?
   d. writing?

Student A	Student B
1. What different languages can you speak? a. b. c.	 a. b. c.
2. What languages do you use a. at home? b. at school? c. at work or school? d. with friends?	 a. b. c. d.
3. What are your favorite activities in a. reading? b. listening? c. talking? d. writing?	 a. b. c. d.

▶ **B** Share the information from your interviews with other people in the class. Find out who

1. speaks the most languages.

   _____

2. uses English at home.

   _____

3. likes to listen to music.

   _____

4. likes to watch movies.

   _____

5. likes to read stories.

   _____

6. likes to surf the Internet.

   _____

7. likes to write letters.

_____

8. likes to talk to people.

_____

▶ **C** Report to the class what you found out.

Writing

▶ **A** Think about reading and speaking in your first language and in English. How do they compare? Write about one of the following topics:

1. What makes reading and speaking easier or more enjoyable in your first language and in English?
2. How many languages do you hear or see in your daily life? Give examples of when you can find more than one language being used, such as signs in airports or government offices.

▶ **B** Summarize for a partner what you wrote about your topic.

Online Study Center   For additional activities, go to the *Reading Matters* Online Study Center a *college.hmco.com/pic/wholeyone2e.*

3 Leave Me a Message

Chapter Openers

Categorizing

▶ **A** Choose Set A below or Set B in the "Exercise Pages" section at the end of the book on page 247.

▶ **B** Read the messages and decide which category each best belongs in. Write W for *work*, *S* for *school*, and *H* for *home*. Some messages might fit in more than one category.

Set A

1. _____ Harry needs your final weekly report today.

2. _____ Don't forget to put out the garbage.

3. _____ We need salsa for the party. Get some on the way home.

4. _____ The librarian called. Your book is overdue. Bring it in tomorrow.

▶ **C** Compare your answers with a partner. Try to agree on the same answers.

▶ **D** Work with a partner who chose the messages in Set B. Take turns reading to each other the messages in both Set A and Set B. Decide which categories your partner's messages belong in.

▶ **E** Write a message of your own for the following people:

Friend: _____

Classmate: _____

Family member: _____

Teacher: _____

▶ Work with a partner to give the messages you wrote.

Discussion Questions

▶ Think about these questions. Share your ideas with a partner or a small group.

1. What is a Post-it® Note? Describe what it looks like.
2. What kind of messages can you write on a Post-it Note?
3. When do you use these notes?
4. Why are Post-it Notes useful?

Exploring and Understanding Reading

Matching

▶ Write the letter of the caption that matches each picture.

1. _____   2. _____   3. _____   4. _____

Captions

a. He needed a bookmark that wouldn't fall out of the book.

b. He put glue on the back edge of the paper. The glue stuck to the pages of the book.

c. He wrote a question on the sticky paper and put it on a report. His boss took the note, wrote an answer, and sent it back.

d. The two men had coffee to celebrate the invention of Post-it Notes.

Predicting

> **Reading Tip**

Predicting the kind of information you might find in a reading will make it easier for you to understand what you read. ■

▶ The following reading is about Post-it Notes. What do you think you could learn from this reading? Check (✔) the information you expect to find in the story.

1. _____ How Post-it Notes were invented

2. _____ Where you can buy Post-it Notes

3. _____ Various uses for Post-it Notes

4. _____ The price of Post-it Notes

▶ Now read the story and put a check beside the ideas that you find.

Notes for Anyone, Anywhere, Anytime

❶   Every day, we have messages to give people. Do you want to tell people about an important meeting? Do you have to leave your office for five minutes? Do you want to remember something important? Write the information on a Post-it Note. Post-it Notes have a special glue on the edge of the paper. They are sticky so that you can leave them anywhere—on a door or on a wall or in a book—and they won't fall out. You can reuse the notes because the special glue on the back doesn't wear off easily, even though it is very light. If you take the note off and put it back down, it will stay in place.

❷   Who invented Post-it Notes? Art Fry was a scientist who worked for the famous 3M Company. He needed a bookmark that stayed in place but didn't tear the page when he wanted to remove it. Then he had an idea. He remembered a friend at the company who was trying to make a special glue. The glue was very weak. It stuck lightly to any surface, and stayed sticky even after you used it. Fry took some of the glue and put it on the back of a yellow piece of paper. Then he wrote a report to his boss and put the yellow sticky paper on the top page. It stayed in place, attached to the report. His boss took off the note, wrote an answer, stuck the paper back on, and sent it back. The two men met for coffee in the cafeteria that afternoon. Fry's boss congratulated him on his invention. This was the beginning of Post-it Notes. In 1980, the company started to distribute the first Post-it Notes in the United States. It was a new and creative way to communicate.

❸   Today, Post-it Notes are one of the most popular office products available. Everyone uses them for many different purposes. One man used it to write a marriage proposal. He wrote, "Will you marry me?" and put the Post-it Note on his girlfriend's front door. She wrote her answer and put the note back on his door. One mother put a note on the back of her son's car before he left on a long trip. When he arrived, he found the note. After 3,000 miles, it was still on the car. One university student was traveling home by bus for the Thanksgiving holiday. She was waiting in the bus terminal and started to feel sleepy. She didn't want to miss her bus so she put Post-it-Notes all over herself. The notes asked people to wake her up in time for her bus. She did fall asleep but her plan worked. Someone saw the notes and woke her up.

❹   There are Post-it Notes to suit everyone's tastes. Now they make super-sticky notes that you can stick on computer monitors or on your household furniture, like the fridge door. And, instead of writing that phone number on your arm, you can even put them on yourself. You can buy Post-it Notes in fifty different colors, twenty-seven different sizes, and fifty-six different shapes. Post-it Notes are popular. More than 400 Post-it products are sold in more than 100 countries around the world. Art Fry should be proud of his invention.

Understanding Details

▶ **A** Circle the letter of the correct answer. In the reading, underline the words that support your answer.

1. People use Post-it Notes for
   a. writing long messages.
   b. writing reports.
   c. writing short messages.

2. You can put a Post-it Note
   a. almost anywhere.
   b. only in books.
   c. only on a wall.

3. Post-it Notes
   a. can be reused.
   b. can't be reused.
   c. can sometimes be reused.

4. Post-it Notes
   a. will stay in place.
   b. will stay in place for a short time.
   c. won't stay in place.

5. Art Fry
   a. made the glue for Post-it Notes.
   b. used the glue a friend made.
   c. made the glue with a friend.

6. Post-it Notes
   a. come in only one color, size, and shape.
   b. come in only a few colors, sizes, and shapes.
   c. come in many colors, sizes, and shapes.

▶ **B** Answer the following questions. In the reading, underline the words that support your answer. Write the question number in the margin.

1. a. What special message did one man used a Post-it Note for?

   _____

   b. What did one mother use a Post-it Note for?

   _____

2. Did the Post-it Notes work for these two people? Explain.

   _____

   _____

3. Why did one university student cover herself in Post-it Notes?

_____

4. How useful was Art Fry's invention?

_____

_____

▶ Work with a partner. Take turns reading the questions and answers to each other. Refer to the reading if you have different answers.

Applying the Information

▶ **A Matching** Use the information from the reading and ideas of your own to match the questions in Column A with the answers in Column B.

Column A

_____ 1. Where and when do you want to meet?

_____ 2. What do you want to talk about?

_____ 3. Can you meet with me today?

_____ 4. Can you ask Jim to make more of that glue?

_____ 5. What do you think the company will say?

Column B

a. Sure, I'm free this afternoon.

b. 3:00 in the cafeteria.

c. I think they'll say that you've invented something very interesting.

d. I've got an idea for a useful new product.

e. Sure, let's call him right away.

▶ Now write the sequence of questions and answers in the correct order on the lines below.

1. _____

2. _____

3. _____

4. _____

5. _____

◐ **B** **Delivering a Message** Two messages were sent to each member of the Armstrong family: John, fifty-five, who is a painter; Nancy, forty-nine, a doctor; Mona, twenty-one, a dancer; and Sam, nineteen, a college student. Work with a partner. Together, read the messages and decide whose box they belong in.

_____ 1. Hi, Dad. I'll be home at 6:00 P.M. Hold supper for me.

_____ 2. Mrs. Brown called. Her arm still hurts. Can you see her? The number is 555-8976.

_____ 3. You have a rehearsal at 8:00. Meet Joe at the studio.

_____ 4. Bob called. He wants you to call him about the test.

_____ 5. Don't worry about supper. I'll pick up a pizza on the way home.

_____ 6. The test is postponed. It won't be until next week.

_____ 7. Don't forget to bring your music to the rehearsal.

_____ 8. The hospital called. The operation will be at 9:00.

◐ Make your own message for each member of the Armstrong family.

◐Vocabulary Building

Word Form and Meaning

◐ **A** Match the words in Column A with their meanings in Column B.

Column A

_____ 1. attach

_____ 2. create

_____ 3. distribute

_____ 4. inform

_____ 5. invent

Column B

a. to tell someone about an idea or an event

b. to make something for the first time

c. to send something to others

d. to make something new

e. to add to or put things together

▶ **B** Study these five words in their various forms: verb, noun, adjective, and adverb. The forms are not in the same order in each column. Then choose the correct form to fill out the chart below. These words are commonly found in general and academic texts.

attach (v.)	create (v.)	distribute (v.)	inform (v.)	invent (v.)
attachment (n.)	creator	distributed	information	inventively
attached (adj.)	creation	distributor	informative	invention
attaching (adj.)	creative	distributive	informed	inventive
	created	distribution	informer	invented
	creatively	distributively	informatively	inventor

Verb	Noun	Adjective	Adverb
create	1.	1.	1.
	2.	2.	
distribute	1.	1.	1.
	2.	2.	
inform	1.	1.	1.
	2.	2.	
invent	1.	1.	1.
	2.	2.	

▶ Compare lists with a partner. Try to agree on the same answers.

▶ **C** Write three sentences using words from the list.

Vocabulary in Context

▶ **A** Complete each sentence with one of the verbs from the following list. Use the words in boldface to help you choose your answer.

a. buy   b. leave   c. remember   d. remove
e. report   f. use   g. write

1. His boss asked him to _____ on the progress of his work **at the weekly departmental meeting.**

2. Did you _____ to go to the meeting, or **did you forget**?

3. You can _____ the notes **in any store** anywhere around the world.

4. He needed **a pen** to _____ a note for her to read.

5. Can you _____ the note in a place **where she will find it?**

6. Can you _____ these papers, **or should I throw them away?**

7. Do you know how to _____ these marks so that **the desks will be clean again?**

▶ **B Prepositions** Write the preposition that best completes the following sentences.

    a. in   b. of   c. off   d. on   e. out   f. for

1. You should take _____ the note after you read the report.

2. Write the message and leave it _____ the door.

3. Put the note _____ where he will see it.

4. Put the note _____ my office door.

5. I'm busy now, but can I speak to you _____ five minutes?

6. I asked her to bring me a box _____ copies _____ the office.

▶ **C Verbs: Present and Past** Write the past form of the following verbs. Check your answers by circling these past tense verbs in the reading.

1. invent _____

2. need _____

3. take _____

4. write _____

5. stick _____

6. meet _____

7. put _____

8. congratulate _____

9. find _____

10. leave _____

▶ Write three sentences and three questions of your own, using both the present and past forms of any of these verbs.

❲Expanding Your Language

Reading

This reading expands on the idea of what we can do with Post-it Notes. Notice how much easier it is to understand this now that you have already done some reading on this topic.

▶ Before beginning, read the following questions. After reading, answer them based on the information in the text.

1. How did Post-it Notes begin and what did they become?
2. How are they being used for playful purposes?
3. What work of art did one professor create?
4. What facts are given about a Canadian art competition?
5. What is one nontraditional use of Post-it Notes reported in a Canadian survey?

Creative Notes

Post-it Notes started out as an experiment and ended up as a practical solution to a problem the inventor had never imagined. These little pieces of paper are now so handy that most people cannot go a day without using one. Now Post-it Notes have even become an art form. What are some of the most unusual uses of Post-it Notes? One group of playful people have started sticking Post-its to their foreheads. Their friends must try to guess what word is written on the back side of the note. Another innovation is a Post-it Art Competition. Vanalyne Green, a professor at the School of the Art Institute of Chicago, won an international prize for her portrait of a cat made from 50,000 Post-it Notes. The idea of art competitions using Post-it Notes is spreading. Recently, students at universities and colleges across Ontario, Canada, took part in a competition sponsored by the 3M Company, the makers of the notes. The winner was given a $5,000 prize. Finally, a survey in Canada asked people what they would do with the last pack of Post-its in the world. More than sixty-one percent answered with nontraditional ideas such as starting a fire or sending messages out to sea in a bottle.

Speaking

▶ **Role Play** Work with a partner. Choose the role of one of the main characters in this chapter's reading, such as Art Fry and his boss or the young man and his fiancée. Together, write out the conversation between the two people, based on the reading and ideas of your own.

Here is one example of how to begin the conversation:

Art: Hi, Jim. I have an idea that I'm working on. I want to talk to you about it. Do you have time to see me?

Jim: Sure, let's go for coffee.

Writing

▶ **Topic Writing** Based on the reading and the other activities in this chapter, prepare to write ten to twelve sentences about the invention and use of Post-it Notes. To do this, make an outline for the ideas you could write about.

Here is a sample outline:

A. What a Post-it Note is
    1. What it looks like (color, size, and so on)
    2. What is special about it
B. Many different uses for a Post-it Note
    1.
    2.
    3.
C. The invention of Post-it Notes
    1.
    2.
    3.

▶ **1.** Write two or three sentences about each idea in your outline. Remember that in written English, a general idea is given in one sentence, and the following sentences give details or examples. Refer to page 26 for some examples.

2. Use your outline to write the information in complete sentences.

3. Work with a partner. Explain to each other the information that you wrote about.

4. Give the paragraph to your teacher.

▶Read On: Taking It Further

Researchers have found that the more you read, the more your vocabulary will increase and the more you will understand. A good knowledge of vocabulary will help you to do well in school and in business.

▶ To find out more about making reading a habit for yourself, answer the following questionnaire.

Questionnaire   ▶ Rank the activities that you think help you to increase the language you understand. Write *1* beside those that help you the most to learn new language, *2* beside those that help you the second most, and so on. If you find two activities that help you equally, write the same number.

_____ Memorizing word lists

_____ Reading texts that are assigned for class

_____ Reading texts that I choose for myself

_____ Talking about the texts that we read for class

_____ Talking about the texts that I choose for myself

_____ Learning how to guess the meaning of words that are new

_____ Doing vocabulary exercises for class reading

_____ Doing extra vocabulary exercises for homework

_____ Studying the dictionary to find out the parts of words

_____ Using the dictionary to look up new words I don't understand

▶ Discuss your questionnaire with a partner. Do not change your answers. Explain the reasons for your rankings and your experiences with reading. Are there other activities that help you to increase your vocabulary? Explain what these are and how they help you.

Reading Journal

An important way to improve your reading skills and to increase your vocabulary is to find material that you choose to read yourself. This activity is called "reading for pleasure." Here are some ideas to start you out.

▶ Find some readings on the topics in this unit that you are interested in and that are at your level. Your teacher can help you to find some stories to read for pleasure. For example, you could choose an easy-reading edition of the life story of Thomas Edison, the inventor of the lightbulb. You could also read the story of Helen Keller, who learned to communicate even though she was blind and deaf.

▶ Another source of reading material is the magazine and newspaper section of your bookstore or library. Discuss with others in a small group what you would like to read. Your group members could recommend something good for you to read. Try to work with a reading partner. Select a reading that your partner will read as well. Make a schedule for the times when you plan to do your personal reading and a time when you would like to finish.

▶ You can use the format outlined in the "Speaking" section that follows to record your notes in your Reading Journal.

Speaking

▶ Be ready to talk with a partner or with others in a small group about what you read. You can complete the following form to help you remember what is important for the others to know.

Reading Journal

Title of the reading: _____

Author: _____

Subject of the reading: _____

_____

Who are the important people in the story?

1. _____

2. _____

3. _____

4. _____

5. _____

What are some of the important ideas?

1. _____

2. _____

3. _____

4. _____

5. _____

Recommendation

This is or isn't good to read, because: _____

1. _____

2. _____

3. _____

4. _____

5. _____

Vocabulary Log

▶ **A** Choose five important words that you learned from each chapter. Write the words and a definition in your notebook. Check your definition with the teacher.

Chapter 1

Word	Definition
1. benefits	some good points
2. _____	_____
3. _____	_____
4. _____	_____
5. _____	_____

…

▶ On a separate page in your notebook, write five sentences. In each sentence, use one of the words you chose.

▶ **B Personal Dictionary** A personal dictionary is a good way to record the new words you learn as you read. To create your dictionary, divide a notebook into sections for each letter of the alphabet. Then, write the word and the definition on the appropriate page. You can also write the way to use the word in a sentence (as a verb, as a noun, as an adjective, as an adverb, or in more than one way). Look for the word in the reading or write the word in a sentence of your own. You can also find synonyms (words that mean the same) or antonyms (words that have an opposite meaning) and write them in your dictionary.

Online Study Center   For additional activities, go to the *Reading Matters* Online Study Center at *college.hmco.com/pic/wholeyone2e.*

The Mysteries of Sleep

Sleep is a reward for some, a punishment for others.

—*Isidore Ducasse*

Introducing the Topic

We all need to sleep, but getting a good night's sleep is not easy for everyone. This unit introduces some ideas and questions about sleep. Chapter 4 shows us that many people today are not getting enough sleep. Why does this happen, and what problems does this cause? In Chapter 5, you'll read about two people and their personal experiences with sleep problems. You'll find out how sleep problems affect their lives. Chapter 6 presents some interesting facts about the subject of dreams.

Points of Interest

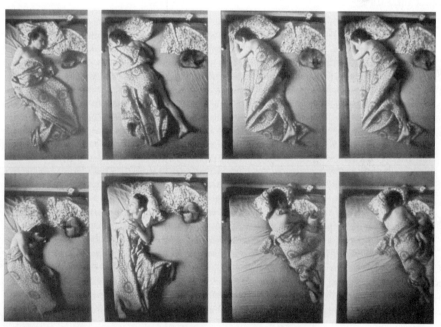

What kind of sleep problem do you think this person is having?

4 Sleep: How Much Is Not Enough?

▶ Chapter Openers

Questionnaire   ▶ Answer these questions for yourself. Then ask two classmates these same questions.

Questions	You	Student A	Student B
1. How many hours a day do you need to sleep?			

2. What time do you
  a. get up?
  b. go to bed?
	a.
	b.
		a.
		b.
			a.
			b.

3. What activities do you do
  a. in the morning?
  b. in the afternoon?
  c. in the evening?
	a.
	b.
	c.
		a.
		b.
		c.
			a.
			b.
			c.

4. Check (✔) the time(s) of the day you feel really tired.	( ) in the morning ( ) in the afternoon ( ) in the evening	( ) in the morning ( ) in the afternoon ( ) in the evening	( ) in the morning ( ) in the afternoon ( ) in the evening
5. How many hours of sleep does a person need as a(n)	baby _____ teenager _____ adult _____ older adult _____	baby _____ teenager _____ adult _____ older adult _____	baby _____ teenager _____ adult _____ older adult _____

▶ Tell the information from your interviews to another person in class.

❯ Exploring and Understanding Reading

Previewing

❯ To preview, follow these steps:

1. Read the title and the first and last sentences of each paragraph in the story.

2. Based on that information, check (✔) from the following list the ideas you expect to find out about in this reading.

1. _____ Why sleep is important to our health

2. _____ Some stories about people with sleep problems

3. _____ Why more people are not getting enough sleep

4. _____ How the need for sleep changes as we get older

5. _____ What kinds of sleep problems are difficult to solve

❯ With a partner, compare your choices. Try to agree on your answers. Then read all of the paragraphs. See whether you should change any of the choices you made.

Sleeping Less in the Twenty-First Century

❶   Today, people are getting less sleep than they need. We need to get 8 hours of sleep each night. But today, many of us are not getting enough hours of sleep. People take time from sleep to do other things. People work longer, go to meetings at night, eat supper late, go food shopping, watch television, spend hours online, or go out until late. Some individuals wake up early to go to the gym, do housework, study, or cook food for later in the day. In today's society, it is easier to do more at night. Some stores stay open 24 hours a day for shopping. Companies want their employees to work more hours and encourage them to work overtime. Television stations broadcast all day and all night. People can stay up to watch TV any time. Many parents come home after a long day and have to spend time taking care of their children. There are many reasons that people today are not getting the sleep they need.

❷   Getting enough sleep is important to your health. When you sleep, your body produces chemicals called hormones. These hormones help the body to rest and to stay healthy. One health problem is weight gain. When you don't get enough sleep, you feel hungry. Your body thinks it needs more calories; it will react even when you have already eaten enough. Another problem is that if you don't get enough sleep, your memory will not work well. You will not be able to concentrate on your work. You will feel worried and in a bad mood. The body uses sleep to make energy for itself. Without enough sleep, you feel tired. When you lose sleep, your body ages at a faster rate. Sleeping reduces the effects of aging.

❸   Our need to sleep changes as we get older. Newborn babies sleep from 16–20 hours a day. Teenagers need about 9 or 10 hours of sleep. Adults need about 8 hours, and the elderly need about 6 or 7. As we age, we lose our ability to sleep. We don't sleep as long or as deeply. Older people can spend a lot of time in bed. But they don't sleep well. It takes them longer to fall asleep, and they don't fall into a deep sleep. Deep sleep is the sleep that refreshes our bodies. Surprisingly, it seems that married people with children and nonsmokers seem to get the best sleep.

❹   Sleep problems can be serious. People with serious sleep problems might need to make an appointment to consult with their doctor or change their lifestyles.

Understanding Details

▶ **A** Circle the letter of the correct answer. In the reading, underline the words that support your answer.

1. People are getting
   a. more sleep than they need.
   b. less sleep than they need.

2. People are doing
   a. more things at night than in the past.
   b. fewer things at night than in the past.

3. Stores stay open
   a. a few hours at night.
   b. all night.

4. When you don't get enough sleep,
   a. your body doesn't produce hormones it needs.
   b. your body produces the hormones it needs.

5. If you don't get enough sleep, you will
   a. lose weight.   b. gain weight.

6. If you don't get enough sleep, you will
   a. remember better and feel happier.
   b. not remember as well or feel as happy.

7. Older people
   a. spend more time in bed but sleep less.
   b. spend less time in bed but sleep more.

▶ **B** Complete the following sentences. In the reading, underline the information that supports your answer.

1. Today, people _____ longer, go to _____, eat late,

   and go _____ shopping at night.

2. People wake up early to go to the _____, do _____,

   study, or _____ food.

3. Your body produces _____ that help you to _____

   and stay _____.

4. When you _____ sleep, your _____ ages.

5. When we get older, we don't get as much _____ sleep.

▶ Work with a partner. Take turns reading the answers. Refer to the reading if you have different answers.

Applying the Information

▶ **Problem Solving** Use the information from the reading and from your own experience to give advice that could solve the following problems. Give as much information in your advice as possible. Include details about how to find time during the day and week, or how to make changes to their schedules. Make a list of ideas to discuss with others.

1. Alice has a full-time job. She works from 8 A.M. to 4 P.M. She is a single mother with two young children. She studies part time in the evening. She feels tired and can't concentrate during the day.

   What is Alice's problem? What are some possible solutions to her problems?

   _____

   _____

   _____

2. Paul is an active university student who does well in school and takes part in a lot of other school activities. He usually goes to bed late and gets up at 7:00 A.M. to get the bus to be in school on time. Lately, he's been spending a lot of his time online, chatting with his friends and discovering some exciting websites. He's staying up later and later. He says that he feels tired most mornings and has even started to miss his bus.

What is Paul's problem? What are some possible ways Paul could solve his problems?

_____

_____

_____

▶ With a partner or with others in a small group, share the list of ideas you made. Present your solutions to the whole class.

Vocabulary Building

Word Form and Meaning

▶ **A** Match the words in Column A with their meanings in Column B.

Column A

_____ 1. concentrate

_____ 2. consult

_____ 3. encourage

_____ 4. react

_____ 5. refresh

Column B

a. to give help or hope to someone

b. to act in answer to someone or something

c. to ask for advice or counsel from an expert

d. to feel new again

e. to fix on an idea or object without losing your focus

▶ **B** Study these five words in their various forms: verb, noun, adjective, and adverb. The forms are not in the same order in each column. Then choose the correct form to fill out the chart on the next page. These words are commonly found in general and academic texts.

concentrate (v.)	consult (v.)	encourage (v.)	react (v.)	refresh (v.)
concentration (n.)	consulting	encouragement	reactive	refreshment
concentrated (adj.)	consultant	encouragingly	reactor	refreshing
concentratedly (adv.)	consultative	encouraging	reaction	refreshed
	consultation	encouraged	reacting	refreshingly

Verb	Noun	Adjective	Adverb
consult	1. 2.	1. 2.	
encourage	1.	1. 2.	1.
react	1. 2.	1. 2.	
refresh	1.	1. 2.	1.

▶ Compare lists with a partner. Try to agree on the same answers.

▶ **C** Write three sentences using words from the list.

Vocabulary in Context

▶ **A** Complete each statement with one of the nouns from the following list. Use the words in boldface to help you choose your answer.

a. ability   b. elderly   c. employees   d. energy
e. memory   f. mood   g. teenagers

1. It takes a lot of _____ **to work all day**.

2. **As we age**, we lose our _____ to sleep.

3. Her _____ was so bad that **she couldn't remember my name**.

4. It is **difficult to be with** him when he is in a bad _____.

5. Why do these _____ seem t**o sleep all day**: from 2 A.M. until 2 P.M.?

6. The _____ have a lot of sleep problems **because of their age**.

7. The **company** asked whether all _____ could work until 8 P.M.

▶ **B** Decide whether the word in bold in each sentence is a noun or a verb. Circle *N* for noun or *V* for verb.

1. N   V   We **need** to get 8 hours of sleep.

2. N   V   Our **need** to sleep changes as we get older.

3. N   V   As we **age**, we lose our ability to sleep.

4. N   V   It is difficult to tell her **age**; it could be sixteen or twenty-six.

5. N   V   I have to get a good night's **sleep** tonight.

6. N   V   Can I **sleep** in the big bedroom?

▶ **C Jigsaw Sentences** Match the beginning of each sentence (Column A) with the ending that fits best (Column B).

Column A

_____ 1. When you sleep

_____ 2. If you don't get enough sleep,

_____ 3. People with serious sleep problems

_____ 4. In today's society,

_____ 5. Getting enough sleep

Column B

a. is important to your health.

b. might need to see a doctor.

c. your body produces hormones.

d. it is easier to do more at night.

e. your memory will not work well.

▶ Compare your answers with a partner. Then take turns reading your answers.

★ Expanding Your Language

Reading

This reading expands on the idea of what we need to get a good night's sleep. Notice how much easier it is to understand this now that you have already done some reading on this topic.

▶ Before beginning, read the following questions. After reading, answer them based on the information in the text.

1. How many adults have trouble sleeping?

2. What is the most common sleep problem people have?

3. How quickly should people be able to get to sleep?

4. What should people do to get a good night's sleep?

5. What should you do if you can't get to sleep quickly?

Sleep Tips

Some researchers say that up to forty percent of adults have trouble sleeping on any given night. Almost half of those people suffer from some kind of sleep problem. Insomnia is the most common problem, but there are, in fact, more than eighty different sleep problems. The experts say you should be able to go to sleep within about ten minutes. If you are having trouble getting to sleep or staying asleep, here are some tips that will help.

1. Have a routine. Go to bed at the same time every night and get up at the same time every morning, even on weekends.
2. Exercise regularly. Working out releases stress and makes you more tired. But don't exercise too close to bedtime.
3. Cut down on drinks and other substances that are stimulants. Coffee, tea, soft drinks, chocolate, and cigarettes all make it hard to sleep.
4. Watch what you eat. Sleeping on a full stomach is difficult.
5. Sleep on a good bed.
6. If you can't get to sleep after ten minutes or so, get up. Have a warm bath or read a book until you feel sleepy.

Speaking

▶ **Questions and Answers** Write five questions about the topic of sleep. Write three questions using question words and two yes/no questions. Use the information in the reading to help you find ideas for questions. Check your questions with your teacher. Then use your questions to interview two people in class. Ask your questions, and in note form, write the answers you receive.

Sample Questions

1. Why do teenagers need to sleep more than older people?
2. In the future, will people work longer or shorter hours?
3. When do you feel the most tired?
4. Is it a good idea to take a nap during the day?

▶ Discuss the information from your interviews with others in a small group.

Writing

▶ Write answers to three of the most interesting questions you prepared. Then work with a partner and report the questions and answers you wrote.

 *Online Study Center*   For additional activities, go to the *Reading Matters* Online Study Center at *college.hmco.com/pic/wholeyone2e.*

5 Sleep Problems

Chapter Openers

Discussion Questions

▷ **Tossing and Turning** Think about these questions. Share your ideas with a partner or in a small group.

1. Do you ever have trouble sleeping?
2. What do you do when you can't sleep?
3. How do you feel when you don't get enough sleep?
4. What are some kinds of sleep problems?
5. How can people solve their sleep problems?

Paired Readings

▷ In this section, you will find two different stories on the same theme. Choose one of the stories to read. Prepare to explain the story to someone who read the same story and then to a person who read the other story.

These are the stories of two people who are having trouble getting a good night's sleep. They are writing to a newspaper column doctor who gives advice to the newspaper's readers. Read and find out about their problems and what the doctor suggests.

▷ Choose one of the stories to read. Work with a partner who is reading the same story.

1 How Snoring Ruined One Woman's Life

Understanding Details

▷ Read each paragraph and then answer the questions. In the paragraph, underline the words that support your answers.

Ask Dr. Snow

Ann's Sleep Problem

❶   Dear Dr. Snow,

My husband, Bob, sleeps very soundly. He gets eight hours of sleep and wakes up feeling great. He is rested and ready for the day. He is usually in a good mood in the morning. I am not so lucky. I can fall asleep, but then I get only three hours of sleep. Why? The reason is that my husband snores. He snores so loudly that it wakes me up. Then I can't get to sleep again. I try to move him onto his side, but after a while, he moves onto his back. Then the snoring begins again. Sometimes, I move to the couch to get some sleep. But often, he is snoring so loudly that I can hear him from the living room. I never get enough sleep.

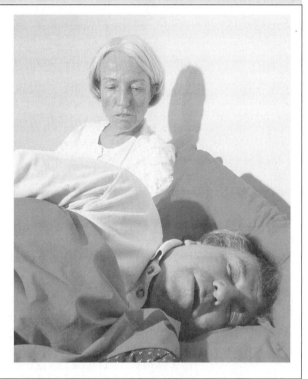

1. How many hours does Bob sleep?

   _____

2. How does he feel in the morning?

   _____

3. How many hours of sleep does Ann get?

   _____

4. What does Ann's husband do?

   _____

5. What does Ann sometimes do?

   _____

6. What can Ann still hear from the living room?

   _____

❷   When I don't get enough sleep, I am in a bad mood. I feel tired and grumpy when I wake up. I am very sleepy in the afternoon. Yesterday, at work, I was at a very long meeting. There were about twenty people around the table. It felt very hot. I had a headache. I closed my eyes for a moment. The next thing I knew, my boss was calling my name. She looked angry. Did I fall asleep? I was so embarrassed. Now I'm afraid of losing my job. What do I do?

1. How does Ann feel when she wakes up?

_____

2. How does she feel in the afternoon?

_____

3. Where was she yesterday?

_____

4. How did she feel at the meeting?

_____

5. What happened to her when she closed her eyes?

_____

6. What is Ann afraid of?

_____

The Doctor's Answer

❸   Dear Ann,
      To help you and your husband, I need to find out more. Is your husband overweight? Does he smoke? Is he very tired? These are some things that can cause snoring. They aren't good for his health. If the answer to any of these questions is yes, he should change his habits. What about the mattress on your bed? Is it very soft? Get a good, medium-strong mattress to sleep on, and make sure that the room is cool. If this doesn't work, there are other methods, such as surgery or a special breathing mask.

1. What questions does the doctor ask about Ann's husband?

   a. _____

   b. _____

   c. _____

2. Should Ann's husband change his habits? Why?

   _____

3. What kind of mattress should Ann get to prevent snoring?

   _____

4. What other methods are there to solve the problem of snoring?

   a. _____

   b. _____

▶ Work with a partner. Take turns reading the questions and answers to each other. Refer to the reading if your answers are different.

Recapping the Story

▶ Reread the first paragraph quickly. Cover the information and tell your partner as much as you can remember. Ask for help if you forget or give incorrect information. Take turns reading and telling the information in all of the paragraphs.

Reacting to the Story

▶ Discuss these questions with a partner.

1. Do you think that Ann might lose her job because of her sleep problem? Why or why not?

2. What do you think that Ann and her husband should do to resolve this situation?

▶ Compare your answers with others in a small group. Choose the most interesting answer to present to others in your class.

❷ Sleeping All Day and Staying Up All Night

Understanding Details ▷ Read each paragraph and then answer the questions. In the paragraph, underline the words that support your answers.

Ask Dr. Snow

Jonathan's Sleep Cycle Problem

❶   Dear Dr. Snow,

I'm an eighteen-year-old student and I'm just beginning my first year at junior college. I graduated from high school, but my grades were not great. All through high school, I had trouble getting up in the morning to get to school on time. I couldn't concentrate in class during the day. My parents tried to force me to sleep for 10 hours every night, but I just couldn't. Now I am worried that I won't be able to succeed in school. I still have trouble staying awake during the day. In fact, I get so tired that I fall asleep in class. One time I felt so exhausted that I fell asleep in my chair during class. Then at night, I cannot fall asleep, even at one or two in the morning.

1. How old is Jonathan?

   _____

2. Where is he going to school now?

   _____

3. What problems did he have during high school?

   _____

4. Why is he worried now?

   _____

5. What happened to him during class?

   _____

6. What happens to him at night?

_____

❷   At night I feel completely awake so I decided on an approach for getting my work done. I go on the Internet. I spend hours online. I do research for my class assignments and get all my homework done. In fact, doing schoolwork online at night was the main reason I didn't fail high school. I had a few teachers who put up their class notes online so that I could go over the information I didn't get during the day. I could continue to do this but I feel that it's not normal to be so tired during the day. I didn't have much of a social life with other students when I was in high school. I would like to make friends with people in college. I would like to feel more awake during the day. What should I do?

1. What does he do at night?

_____

2. How does his work at night affect his school performance?

_____

3. What does he feel about how he feels during the day?

_____

4. What would he like to be able to do in college that he could not do during high school?

_____

5. What would he like to be able to do during the day?

_____

The Doctor's Answer

❸   Dear Jonathan,

To help you, I would like to know more. How many hours of sleep do you get? When do you feel you could fall asleep? Are you taking any sleep medication? If you feel like you could sleep in the day but not at night, you might have a special sleep problem. It might be that your sleep and wake cycles are the opposite of most people's cycles. Most people feel awake in the day and tired at night. You should make an appointment to see your doctor. Ask your doctor to refer you to a specialist who can test you and find out if you have a sleep disorder that makes it difficult to sleep at night. When you know what the test results indicate, then together with your doctor and family, you can make some plans to change your sleep/wake cycle.

1. What three questions does the doctor ask?

   _____

2. What could be the problem with Jonathan's sleep cycle?

   _____

3. What are most people's sleep cycles like?

   _____

4. What should Jonathan do?

   _____

5. What kind of test should Jonathan ask his doctor to do?

   _____

6. What kind of plans could Jonathan make?

   _____

▶ Work with a partner. Take turns reading the questions and answers to each other. Refer to the reading if you have different answers.

Recapping the Story

▶ Reread the first paragraph quickly. Then cover the information and tell your partner as much as you can remember. Ask for help if you forget or give incorrect information. Take turns reading and telling the information in all of the paragraphs.

Reacting to the Story

▶ Discuss these questions with a partner.

1. Many young adults have trouble waking up on time in the morning. Should schools have classes start later in the morning?
2. What advice would you give to a friend who has a sleep cycle problem? What suggestions would you want to offer?

▶ Compare your answers with others in a small group. Choose the most interesting answer to present to others in your class.

Comparing the Readings

Discussing the Stories

▶ **A** Work with a partner who read a different story. Tell your partner the details of the story you read. Then listen to your partner's story. With your partner, tell back the story you heard. Finally, discuss the questions in the "Reacting to the Story" section of both readings.

▶ **B** Work with a partner. Circle *T* for true or *F* for false. If the answer is false, tell your partner the correct information.

1. T F   Both of the people in these stories have the same sleep problem.

2. T F   Ann and Jonathan are both tired during the day.

3. T F   Ann and Jonathan are both very busy during the day.

4. T F   Ann and Jonathan are both worried about the reactions of the people they meet.

5. T F   Ann and Jonathan are both worried about their social lives.

6. T F   Ann and Jonathan both ask a doctor for advice.

7. T F   Ann and Jonathan get similar advice for their problems.

Applying the Information

▶ **Problem Solving** Based on the information in the chapter readings and your own ideas, what advice would you give to these people? Follow these steps.

▶ **1.** Discuss the situation with a partner. What problem does the person have?

2. Make a list of three to five suggestions you could give. Include suggestions about what the person should or could do or not do. For example: You should make sure that the bedroom is quiet and comfortable. You shouldn't drink any coffee at night. You could try to take a nap during the afternoon.

1. Paul, a student from another country, is studying in your class. Paul tells you that he is having a hard time going to bed before 2:00 or 3:00 in the morning. He likes to study late at night and then watches the late-night movie. Sometimes, he watches TV all night. The television is in his bedroom. Then in the morning, he can't get up. Paul wants your advice.

Your Advice

_____

_____

2. Joan is a college student. She works part time to pay for her expenses. She works during the week from 6:00 until 11:00 four nights a week. Joan comes

home at around midnight, and then she studies until 3:00 in the morning. On the weekend, she sleeps late to catch up on her sleep. Now her boss has told her that he needs someone to work Saturday and Sunday from 7:00 A.M. until 3:00 P.M. Joan is worried that she won't get enough sleep, but she doesn't want to lose her job. Joan wants your advice.

Your Advice

_____

_____

▶Vocabulary Building

Word Form and Meaning

▶ **A** Match the words in Column A with their meanings in Column B.

Column A

_____ 1. approach

_____ 2. embarrass

_____ 3. indicate

_____ 4. medicate

_____ 5. worry

Column B

a. to give medicine

b. to feel concern

c. to come close to or do something in a special way

d. to show something

e. to cause someone discomfort

▶ **B** Study these five words in their various forms: verb, noun, adjective, and adverb. The forms are not in the same order in each column. Then choose the correct form to fill out the chart on the next page. These words are commonly found in general and academic texts.

approach (v.)	embarrass (v.)	indicate (v.)	medicate (v.)	worry (v.)
approach (n.)	embarrassment	indication	medically	worry
approachability (n.)	embarrassing	indicated	medicating	worrier
approachable (adj.)	embarrassed	indicative	medicated	worried
approaching (adj.)	embarrassingly	indicator	medication	worrying
		indicatively	medical	
			medicator	

Verb	Noun	Adjective	Adverb
embarrass	1.	1.	1.
		2.	
indicate	1.	1.	1.
	2.	2.	
medicate	1.	1.	1.
	2.	2.	
		3.	
worry	1.	1.	
	2.	2.	

▶ Compare lists with a partner. Try to agree on the same answers.

▶ **C** Write three sentences using words from the list.

Vocabulary in Context

▶ **A** Complete each statement with one of the adjectives from the following list. Use the words in boldface to help you choose your answer.

a. angry   b. comfortable   c. embarrassed   d. grumpy   e. health
f. lucky   g. quiet   h. sleepy   i. strong

1. I think he was _____ because **I fell asleep while he was talking**.

2. I asked **the doctor to give me advice** about my _____ problems.

3. When you are in **a bad mood**, it makes me feel _____ too.

4. The bed was so soft and _____ that **I fell asleep very quickly**.

5. **No one is at home** today, so the house is very _____.

6. I felt so _____ that I couldn't remember her name **that my face turned red**.

7. He's very _____ that **he can sleep anywhere even if it's noisy**.

8. I like to drink very _____ **coffee when I have to stay awake**.

9. **I stayed up all night**, so today I feel so _____ that I can't study.

▶ **B** **Jigsaw Sentences** *But* is a word that shows a contrasting or a conditional idea. *But* usually joins two parts of a sentence. For example: Jonathan wants to sleep at night, *but* he feels completely awake. Use your understanding of the ideas to complete these sentences.

▶ Match the beginning of each sentence (Column A) with the ending that fits best (Column B).

Column A

_____ 1. He tries to sleep on his side,

_____ 2. He wants to get up early for school,

_____ 3. I try not to worry,

_____ 4. She spends a lot of time in bed,

_____ 5. He called her name,

Column B

a. but she didn't hear him.

b. but she doesn't sleep well.

c. but it's difficult to forget about daily problems.

d. but he often stays up late watching movies all night.

e. but he often moves onto his back.

▶ Compare your answers with a partner. Then take turns reading your answers.

▶ **C** **Categorizing** In each of the following groups, circle the word that does not belong. Prepare to explain the reason for your choice.

1. tired   awake   sleepy   grumpy

2. often   sleep   always   sometimes

3. snoring   smoking   cool   worrying

4. stress   pain   headache   coffee

5. desk   bed   couch   living room

▶ **Pair Work** Tell your partner your answer and the reason why it doesn't belong.

D Antonyms Antonyms are two words that have opposite meanings, such as *hot* and *cold*. Match each word or phrase in Column A with its antonym in Column B.

Column A

_____ 1. loudly

_____ 2. wake up

_____ 3. worried

_____ 4. embarrassed

_____ 5. everything

_____ 6. quiet

_____ 7. problems

_____ 8. rested

_____ 9. continue

_____10. open

Column B

a. close

b. carefree

c. solutions

d. stop

e. noisy

f. fall asleep

g. nothing

h. proud

i. softly

j. tired

▶ €xpanding Your Language

Speaking

A Role Play Work with a partner. Choose the role of one of the people in one of the stories. Based on the ideas in the story and ideas of your own, write out a conversation. You may want to add characters, such as Ann's husband or boss or Jonathan's friends or parents, to the story.

Here is one example of how to begin the conversation.

Ann: Doctor, I have a terrible problem. My husband wakes me up. He snores and I can't sleep.

Doctor: Well, tell me a little more. How often do you wake up at night?

▶ Use your lines to act out the story, but you do not have to memorize the lines. You can be creative and improvise if you need to.

B Two-Minute Taped Talk Record a two-minute audiotape or audio CD about one of the stories in this chapter. To make your recording, follow these steps.

▶ **1.** Choose one of the stories to talk about.

2. Reread the story.

3. In note form, write the information that you remember. Include as many of the important facts of the story as possible.

4. Refer to the reading and check your notes for information that you left out or that was incorrect. Make any necessary changes.

5. Practice telling the story a few times until you can speak without reading what you wrote.

6. Time yourself as you try to speak as clearly and naturally as possible.

7. Record yourself telling the story.

8. Give the recording to your teacher for feedback.

Writing

▶ Write a sentence of your own, based on the definitions of these sleep expressions.

1. **Sleep in: to get up later than you usually would.** *Example:* I was up until 2:00 A.M., so I decided to **sleep in** until 11:00 A.M. today.

   _____

   _____

2. **Sleep on: to think about something before doing it.** *Example:* He wants me to go out with him, but I told him I wanted to **sleep on** it.

   _____

   _____

3. **Sleep over: to spend the night at someone else's home.** *Example:* She asked five of her friends to **sleep over** at her house after the party.

   _____

   _____

4. **Sleeping bag: a warm, lined bag used to keep warm when sleeping outdoors or away from home.** *Example:* I brought my **sleeping bag** for the camping trip.

   _____

   _____

 **Online Study Center**   For additional activities, go to the *Reading Matters* Online Study Center at *college.hmco.com/pic/wholeyone2e.*

6 Why Do We Dream?

Chapter Openers

Discussion Questions

▶ **The World of Our Dreams** Think about these questions. Share your ideas with a partner or in a small group.

1. How often do you think you dream?
2. What dreams do you remember?
3. Do you ever
   a. dream in color?
   b. dream in another language?
   c. dream about traveling to distant places?
   d. dream about people you know?
   e. find that your dreams come true?
   f. find answers to the problems you are working on or thinking about?
4. Do you think that dreams have special meanings?

▶ Explain your answers by giving as many examples and ideas as you can.

Getting Information from Illustrations

▶ Look at the illustration and answer these questions.

1. How many REM cycles do we have in one night?
2. What REM cycle lasts the longest?

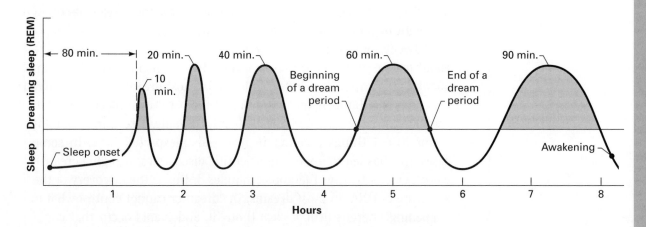

⟨€xploring and Understanding Reading

Previewing

⟩ Read the title and the first sentence of each paragraph in the reading. Based on that information, check (✔) the ideas you expect to find out about in this reading.

1. _____ The common ideas in dreams

2. _____ The cycles and stages of dreaming

3. _____ Stories about the dreams people have

4. _____ How dreaming changes as we get older

⟩ Compare your choices with a partner. Try to agree on your answers. Then read all of the paragraphs. Check to see whether you should change any of the choices you made.

The Mystery of Dreams

❶   Do you remember your dreams? Do people have the same dreams? Why do we dream? There are many questions about dreams. Sleep researchers know we dream during the REM (rapid eye movement) stage of sleep. We have about five periods of REM sleep during the night. The first REM cycle lasts about 10 minutes. As the night goes on, the REM cycle gets longer. By early morning, the REM cycle can last up to 90 minutes. Usually, it is in this last REM cycle that we remember our dreams.

❷   Research has revealed a wealth of information about dreams. First, dreams change as people age. Infants dream about half of the time they are asleep. But, of course, we don't know what it is they dream about. At age eight or nine, children start to tell their dreams as stories. People aged twenty-one to thirty-four report that many of their dreams are about feeling guilty for things that they did. Older men usually dream about work or their families. People see in most dreams, and they may also hear, smell, touch, and taste in them. Most dreams occur in color, though the color is often recalled only vaguely. Dreaming thought seems to put things together in new and unexpected ways. In some cases, this has led to important scientific discoveries or highly creative works. One of the most famous examples of this is the discovery of the structure of DNA. In most dreams, the dreamer cannot control what is happening, there is little logical thought, and events occur that could not happen in real life. Occasionally, the dreamer will realize that he or she is dreaming and may be able to alter what happens in the dream. This is called a lucid dream.

❸   Many dreams share common ideas and concerns. Some common dreams are about falling, flying, or floating in the sky. In many dreams, people forget something important, such as going to work on time or putting on clothes. In many dreams, people miss their bus, plane, or train, or they are late for an appointment. Most people's dreams have two other people in them. Bad dreams are more common than good ones. When people are in trouble, they often have negative dreams. People who are widowed or divorced dream about death more often than married people do. More women than men talk about their dreams. Some people think that our dreams help us to find solutions to problems we're thinking about. For example, one artist was looking for a special design to use for a piece of jewelry. She spent weeks trying to create the design, but nothing worked. She went to sleep thinking about her problem. When she woke up, she remembered dreaming about the design she was looking for.

❹   Do you want to remember your dreams? If you wake up during a dream, you will remember it better. Also, if you wake up without an alarm, you will remember your dreams better. If you want to, you can train yourself to remember your dreams. One way is to tell yourself that you will remember your dream right before you go to sleep. Then ask yourself what your dream was when you first wake up. Keep a pen and paper or a tape recorder near your bed, and write or record what you dreamed about. When people are worried, they don't remember their dreams very well.

❺   We never stop dreaming. But we can't really say what dreams mean or how they happen. Dreams are still a mystery.

Understanding Details

▶ **A** Circle *T* for true and *F* for false. In the reading, underline the words that provide support for your answers. Correct any information that is false.

1. T F   We dream during the REM stage of sleep.

2. T F   We have only three periods of REM sleep during the night.

3. T F   As the night goes on, the REM cycles get shorter.

4. T F   Our dreams stay the same throughout our lives.

5. T F   We usually dream in color.

6. T F   Some important scientific discoveries have occurred to people in their dreams.

7. T F   Many people have dreams about ordinary things that could happen to them.

8. T F   Most people's dreams have other people in them.

9. T F   Good dreams are more common than bad dreams.

10. T F   A bad dream could be a sign of trouble in a person's life.

11. T F   Women report their dreams more often than men do.

12. T F   People can learn how to remember their dreams.

▶ **B** Answer the following questions.

1. How much of their sleep time do infants spend dreaming?

_____

2. How do children tell about their dreams?

_____

3. What kinds of dreams do people aged twenty-one to thirty-four have?

_____

4. What do older men dream about?

_____

5. What is a lucid dream?

_____

6. What important things do people dream they forget to do?

_____

7. What kinds of things do people dream they miss?

_____

8. Why is it useful to think about a problem before going to sleep?

_____

9. When will you better remember your dreams?

_____

10. How can you remember your dreams?

_____

11. When is it difficult for people to remember their dreams?

_____

▶ Work with a partner. Take turns reading the questions and answers. Refer to the reading if you have different answers.

Evaluating the Information

▶ Use the information from the reading to decide who is speaking. The choices include

a. a sleep expert.
b. the mother of an infant.
c. an eight-year-old child.
d. a twenty-four-year-old person.
e. an older man.

▶ On the line after each statement, write the letter of the speaker. Give reasons to explain your choice, based on the reading.

1. I can't believe that she is dreaming. She's so young. What can she be dreaming about? But I can see that her eyes are moving back and forth. _____

2. I had a dream that I was talking with you and Harry. We were trying to finish the work on our project, but we couldn't find the last part of it. We looked everywhere without success. _____

3. I had a dream that I forgot your birthday present and didn't have anything to give you. I felt really bad, and I didn't know what I would say to you. _____

4. In my dream, there was a park. And we decided to play there. We took off our shoes to play in the sand. Then it started to rain, and I couldn't find my shoes. _____

5. Sleep research tells us that we dream during the REM stage of sleep. There are about five of these stages during a night of sleep. _____

▶ Compare your answers with a partner. Try to agree on the same answers. Take turns reading the statements and telling the identity of the speaker.

❶Vocabulary Building

Word Form and Meaning

▶ **A** Match the words in Column A with their meanings in Column B.

Column A

_____ 1. cycle

_____ 2. design

_____ 3. occur

_____ 4. research

_____ 5. reveal

Column B

a. to study or look into a problem

b. to happen or take place

c. to show something new or surprising

d. to make a plan for something such as a building

e. to pass through a period of time; a long period of time

▶ **B** Study these five words in their various forms: verb, noun, adjective, and adverb. The forms are not in the same order in each column. Then choose the correct form to fill out the chart below. These words are commonly found in general and academic texts.

cycle (v.)	design (v.)	occur (v.)	research (v.)	reveal (v.)
cycles (n.)	designer	occurrence	research	revealingly
cyclist (n.)	designing	occurring	researcher	revealed
cycled (adj.)	designed	occurred	researched	revelation
cyclical (adj.)	design		research	revealing
cyclically (adv.)				

Verb	Noun	Adjective	Adverb
design	1.	1.	
	2.	2.	
occur	1.	1.	
		2.	
research	1.	1.	
	2.	2.	
reveal	1.	1.	1.
		2.	

▶ Compare lists with a partner. Try to agree on the same answers.

▶ **C** Write three sentences using words from the list.

▶ **D** Many words have more than one form. Look at the different forms for the word *research*.

a. **research (noun):** a careful investigation or experimentation
b. **research (adjective):** related to an investigation or experiment
c. **research (verb):** to investigate or test

▶ Read the sentences below and write the letter of the correct form on the line provided.

1. _____ He brought all of his **research** with him to show his professor.

2. _____ She was a part of a **research** team to test the new sleep technique.

3. _____ Could you **research** this for our team?

4. _____ The **research** project was completed yesterday.

5. _____ They did the **research** for his article on sleep problems.

6. _____ Scientists often **research** the effects of sleeplessness on people's moods.

▶ **E Verbs: Present and Past** Write the past form of the following verbs. Circle these past tense verbs in the reading.

1. divorce   _____

2. forget   _____

3. lead   _____

4. recall   _____

5. remember   _____

6. spend   _____

7. worry   _____

▶ Compare your answers with a partner. Write three sentences and three questions of your own, using both the present and past forms of any of these verbs.

Vocabulary in Context

▶ Complete each statement with one of the nouns or verbs from the following list. Use the words in boldface to help you choose your answer.

a. appointment	b. change	c. divorced	d. dream	e. forget	f. report
g. remember	h. share	i. train	j. wake up	k. widowed	l. worried

1. They were _____ **after five years of marriage, because they were unhappy**.

2. You have to _____ at 7:00 if you want **to get to school on time**.

3. I wanted to _____ what she said **because it was important**.

4. When people are _____, they **don't sleep very well**.

5. **Last night**, I had a strange _____ about my grandparents.

6. **As people get older**, they _____ in many different ways.

7. I have an _____ to see **him at 9:00, and I don't want to be late**.

8. I never _____ my dreams, because **I tell myself to remember** before I go to sleep.

9. She was _____, and it was difficult for her to enjoy life **without her husband**.

10. I have **to travel** by _____ if I want to visit her.

11. She asked everyone to _____ what he or she saw **so that everyone would know what happened**.

12. **We are similar** in that we _____ a love for languages.

Expanding Your Language

Reading

This reading expands on the topic of dreams. Notice how much easier it is to understand this now that you have already done some reading on the subject.

▶ Before beginning, read the following questions. After reading, answer them based on the information in the text.

1. What is a dream?
2. What are dreams related to?
3. What kinds of dreams can people have?
4. Who was Sigmund Freud and why is he famous?
5. What did Patricia Garfield discover about the common dream types?
6. Why do some people want to understand their dreams?
7. What do psychotherapists do?

The Meaning of Dreams

A dream is a story that a person "watches" or appears to take part in during sleep. Dream events are imaginary, but they are related to real experiences in the dreamer's life. They seem real to the dreamer while they are taking place. Some dreams are pleasant, others are annoying, and still others are frightening. Sigmund Freud was one of the first people to look seriously at dreams. He was an Austrian doctor. He was the father of Western psychology. He developed one of the best-known theories of the meaning of dreams or dream interpretation.

Since Freud, many people have studied dreams. They have found that dreams have some common elements. One woman, Patricia Garfield, has made a list of the twelve most common dreams that appear in many different generations and cultures. The following is a list of these dream types. Each type has a positive and a negative side.

Negative	Positive
1. Being chased or attacked	Being loved or hugged
2. Being injured or dying	Being reborn or healed
3. Having car trouble	Having fun in your car
4. Having damage to your house	Improving your house
5. Doing poorly on a test	Doing great on a test
6. Falling or drowning	Flying or dancing
7. Having no clothes or the wrong clothes on	Getting new clothes
8. Missing your ride	Taking a great trip
9. Bad telephone connection	Good telephone connection
10. Natural disaster	Natural beauty
11. Being lost	Discovering a new place
12. Being bothered by a ghost	Being helped by a ghost

Scientists don't completely understand why we dream. Some people don't think that their dreams have any special meaning. But other people feel that they do. They believe that their hidden feelings come to the surface in dreams. Psychotherapists interpret peoples' dreams in order to help them understand themselves better.

Speaking

▶ **Discussion Questions** People all over the world dream. Do different cultures see dreams and dreaming differently? Get together in a small group with people from different countries or from different parts of the world. Find out from one another the following things:

1. What different kinds of dreams do people have?
2. What are the meanings of dreams?
3. What stories or myths are there about dreams and their meanings?
4. What are some examples of happy dreams, scary dreams, dreams that tell the future, and dreams that occur more than once?

Writing

▶ **Topic Writing** From the ideas in the chapter and your own experience, write ten to fifteen sentences about the topic of dreams. To do this, follow these steps:

▶ **1.** Use the following outline to help yourself make a few notes before you begin to write.

▶ **Write some facts about when people dream.**

The sleep cycle

a. REM _____

_____

b. _____

_____

How long does each cycle last?

First: _____

Second: _____

Third: _____

Fourth: _____

Fifth: _____

How does it change as people get older?

_____

_____

_____

▶ **Write some facts about the types of dreams people have.**

1. _____

_____

2. _____

_____

3. _____

_____

▶ **Write some facts about how to remember dreams.**

1. _____

_____

2. _____

_____

3. _____

_____

▶ **2.** Work with a partner. Use your outline to help you tell your partner what you plan to write about. Listen to your partner's outline of ideas. Compare the two outlines. Make any changes you need to improve your outline.

3. Write as much as you can. Write in complete sentences. Use your notes to help you write.

▶Read On: Taking It Further

Reading Cloze   ▷ Use the words from the unit listed here to fill in the blanks in this paragraph.

a. asleep (2×)   b. awake (2×)   c. breathing   d. dreaming
e. enough   f. feels   g. hours   h. longer
i. need   j. remember   k. sleep (2×)

What happens when we (1) _____? When we fall (2) _____,

our brain and body activity decreases. Our heartbeats and (3) _____

get slower. Our brain waves get slower and (4) _____ or deeper.

This sleep takes place during the first (5) _____ after we fall

(6) _____. As we continue to sleep, our brains send out small,

fast waves similar to when we are (7) _____. Our eyes are moving

under the eyelids. This shows that we are (8) _____. We usually

(9) _____ the last dream of the night. Normally, people

(10) _____ 7–10 hours of (11) _____ each night. But

many of us are not getting (12) _____ sleep. Without sleep, a

person (13) _____ tired and has difficulty thinking and staying

(14) _____. But getting a good night's sleep solves these problems.

▷ Compare your answers with a partner. Try to agree on the same answers.

Reading Suggestions

▷ Ask your teacher to suggest a story or an article to read on the topic of sleep and dreams.

> **Reading Tip**

Don't forget to write in your **reading journal** and enter new words for this chapter in your **vocabulary log**. Show your journal and log entries to your teacher. ■

Sample suggestion: Dreamcatchers are common in North American Indian culture. They are objects that look like a spider's web. They are hung near where a person sleeps. They are meant to catch bad dreams before they can enter a person's mind. Read about dreamcatchers or other dream customs from different cultures.

Word Play

▶ **A Spelling Game** You can use vocabulary from the chapter readings to play this game. Think of a pair of words, such as *dream* and *mystery*. The last letter of *dream* (m) is the first letter of *mystery*. Select a partner and follow these rules to play the game.

▶ **1.** From the reading, make a list of seven to ten words that can be paired with another word.

2. Give your partner the first word to spell.

3. Your partner spells the word and then must select a new word that begins with the last letter of the word spelled (time limit: 1 minute). You must spell this word. If your partner can't find a word, you supply an answer, and your partner continues to spell.

4. Continue to take turns until the teacher calls time (after about 10 minutes).

5. The pair that correctly chooses and spells the most words wins.

 *Online Study Center*   For additional activities, go to the *Reading Matters* Online Study Center at *college.hmco.com/pic/wholeyone2e.*

Relationships

Every community
has its own
customs and
traditions.

—*Philippine Proverb*

Introducing the Topic

We meet people every day. People have many different kinds of relationships with one another. These relationships can be easy or difficult, long or short. As we make contact with various people, our lives change. This unit touches on some of the types of relationships people enjoy. Chapter 7 looks at some dating customs now and in the past. In Chapter 8, you'll read about the ways people can improve their relationships. Chapter 9 focuses on the ways neighbors are meeting to help one another out.

Points of Interest

What kind of relationship do you think these people have?

Is Dating Still the Same?

Chapter Openers

Discussion Questions

▶ **Dating Customs** Think about these questions. Share your ideas with a partner or in a small group.

1. What is a date? What does it mean to go on a date?
2. Why do people go on dates? Do or did you ever go on dates?
3. Where are some good places to go and good things to do on a date?
4. How much money do you usually spend on a date?
5. Who usually asks for a date: the man, the woman, or either?
6. How is dating today different from dating in the past
   a. in the United States?
   b. in other countries?

Exploring and Understanding Reading

Predicting

▶ This is an interview with a twenty-year-old man and a fifty-eight-year-old woman about the way dating today is different from the way it was in the past. What questions do you think that David, the interviewer, will ask? Write three questions.

1. _____

2. _____

3. _____

▶ With a partner, compare your questions. Then quickly read the interview. Check (✔) any of the predicted questions you find.

Dating: What's Changed and What Hasn't

David: They say that in the 1970s, you could meet people to date at bars; in the 1980s, at health clubs; and in the 1990s, at bookstores. I want to find out about the differences between dating now and the way it was in the 1960s. Susan Harding, fifty-eight, and Jerry Brown, twenty, are here with me today. Let me ask you both this question: Where would you go to meet an individual you'd like to date?

Susan: Well, I didn't start to date until I was sixteen. In my day, there were lots of places to go and meet someone interesting. I went to school dances, ball games, church activities, and summer camp; camp was the best.

Jerry: Well, it's not as easy to meet people today. Sometimes, I meet people at work or at the gym. I know one person who met someone through a personal ad in the newspaper. Some people end up going to bars or clubs to meet people, but that's not for me. Then there's the Internet. I think that it's hard to actually get to know someone through the Internet. You can't be sure if the other person is being honest with you.

Susan: We didn't have the Internet, but we did have blind dates. A friend would arrange for you to go out with someone you didn't know at all—a stranger. Sometimes, it worked out. My brother met his wife on a blind date.

David: Suppose you meet someone you like. Who does the asking: the man or the woman?

Susan: In my day, the man always asked the woman out.

Jerry: That's not true today. Both men and women ask each other out. It doesn't matter who does the asking.

David: What about clothes? Would you wear something special or get something new to wear?

Jerry: I would. Clothes are expensive, but I like to wear things that make me look good.

Susan: I never spent a lot of time and money on clothes. I hated having to find the money to pay off my bills. Except for when I had a special date, like a formal dance or the senior prom. Then I would buy something special.

David: Who pays for the date?

Jerry: It depends. If I ask someone out, normally I pay. If she asks me out, we usually split the bill.

Susan: Well, usually the man paid. But sometimes we'd "go Dutch"; I paid for my bill, and he'd pay for his.

David: How much would it cost to go out on a typical date?

Susan: In 1966, movie tickets for two people cost about $5.00. Dinner, including wine, for two in a good restaurant cost about $25.00. A dozen roses cost about $7.00. In all, it was about one day's pay.

Jerry: Today, it can cost $100–$130 for movie tickets, dinner in a nice restaurant, and flowers. It's about half a week's pay. But, actually, my idea of a special date is to go somewhere that doesn't cost a lot of money—I like to be economical—somewhere where you can relax and get to know each other. In my neighborhood, there's a local bookstore/café that's really stylish and intimate; that's the best.

Susan: I agree, definitely. My best dates were going to this little coffee shop and sitting for hours, just talking. I believe in this: it doesn't matter where you go, as long as you have a good time. And of course, if you don't find the right person at first, don't give up.

Understanding Details

▶ **A** Circle *T* if the statement is true and *F* if the statement is false. In the reading, underline the words that support your answer. Correct any information that is false.

1. T   F   Today, it is more difficult to meet people you'd like to date.

2. T   F   You could meet someone you liked on a blind date.

3. T   F   In the past, women asked men out on dates.

4. T   F   Susan and Jerry both like to spend time and money on getting the right clothes.

5. T   F   In the past, men usually paid for the cost of a date.

6. T   F   Today, dates are more expensive than in the past.

7. T   F   Susan and Jerry both like dates that don't cost a lot of money.

▶ **B** Answer the following questions. In the reading, circle the parts that support your answer. Write the question number in the margin.

1. Where did Susan go to meet people she could date?

_____

> Reading Tip

Marking the **question number in the margin** of the reading to show where the information is located helps you to find the information more easily and to discuss the answers more completely when you work with your partner. ▇

2. Where does Jerry meet people he could date?

_____

3. When did Susan spend money on clothes for a date?

_____

4. Does Jerry spend money on clothes for a date? Explain.

_____

5. Does Jerry usually pay for a date? Explain.

_____

6. How does the cost of Susan's date in 1966 compare to the cost of Jerry's date today?

_____

7. What is their idea of a special date?

_____

▶ Work with a partner. Read your questions and answers. Refer to the reading if you have different answers.

▶ **C Identifying the Speaker** Who said what? Write the name of the person who said the following.

1. _____ The man asked the woman out.

2. _____ How much would it cost to go out on a date?

3. _____ A dozen roses cost about $7.00.

4. _____ A friend would arrange for you to go out with someone you didn't know at all.

5. _____ Clothes are expensive, but I like to wear clothes that make me look good.

6. _____ Usually, I pay for the date if I ask someone out.

7. _____ Where would you go to meet people you'd like to date?

8. _____ My idea of a special date is to go somewhere that doesn't cost a lot of money.

▶ Compare your answers with a partner. Take turns reading the questions and statements.

Evaluating the Information

▶ **Categorizing** What do Susan and Jerry say? Complete the chart, based on the information you read.

Idea	Susan	Jerry
1. Where to meet people to date:		
2. Who pays for the date:		
3. What it costs:		
4. Suggestion for a special date:		

▶ With a partner, ask and answer questions to compare your charts.

Discussion Questions

▶ **Agree or Disagree?** Based on the information in this chapter and your own experience, circle *A* if you agree or *D* if you disagree with these statements. Work with a partner or others in a small group to share your ideas. Give the reasons for your answers.

1. A D Sixteen is a good age to begin dating.

2. A D Going on a date is a good way to get to know someone.

3. A D Dating is too expensive.

4. A D Parents should know whom their children are dating.

5. A D In the future, dating will disappear.

6. A D When you get older, dating is not as much fun as when you're young.

Vocabulary Building

Word Form and Meaning

▶ **A** Match the words in Column A with their meanings in Column B.

Column A

_____ 1. economize

_____ 2. individualize

_____ 3. normalize

_____ 4. relax

_____ 5. style

Column B

a. to bring something to its usual state

b. to design or make something fashionable

c. to change something to fit a particular person or situation

d. to keep from spending too much money

e. to feel comfortable or at ease

▶ **B** Study these five words in their various forms: verb, noun, adjective, and adverb. The forms are not in the same order in each column. Then choose the correct form to fill out the chart below. These words are commonly found in general and academic texts.

economize (v.)   individualize (v.)   normalize (v.)   relax (v.)   style (v.)
economy (n.)   individual   normally   relaxed   style
economist (n.)   individual   normal   relaxation   styling
economical (adj.)   individualist   normality   relaxing   stylish
economically (adv.)   individually   stylist
                                                                                stylishly

Verb	Noun	Adjective	Adverb
individualize	1. 2.	1.	1.
normalize	1.	1.	1.
relax	1.	1. 2.	
style	1. 2.	1. 2.	1.

▶ Compare lists with a partner. Try to agree on the same answers.

▶ **C** Write three sentences using words from the list.

▶ **D Verbs** Write the past form of the following verbs. Circle the forms of these verbs that you find in the reading.

Present Tense	Past Tense
1. do	_____
2. meet	_____
3. date	_____
4. have	_____
5. work	_____
6. pay	_____
7. cost	_____
8. wear	_____
9. get	_____
10. go	_____

▶ **E** Write two sentences and two questions of your own, using the present and past tenses of the verbs in both the affirmative and negative forms of the verbs.

Vocabulary in Context

▶ **A** Complete each sentence with one of the words from the following list. Use the words in boldface to help you choose your answer.

a. arrange	b. cost	c. dated	d. differences
e. meet	f. split	g. stranger	h. unusual

1. Let's _____ the bill; **you pay half and I'll pay half**.

2. At first, I thought he was a _____, but then I remembered his name and **where we'd met before**.

3. **How much** does the ticket _____?

4. I met **a girl my brother liked** and _____ a few times when he was in high school.

5. Could you _____ for me to be introduced to your brother **before the party begins**?

6. There are so many _____ between them; they have **nothing in common**.

7. Hello, it's so nice to finally _____ you after **hearing so much about you**.

8. It's so _____ to find **anyone who likes this kind of music**.

▶ **B Matching** Match each phrase in Column A with the word or phrase that is closest in meaning in Column B. Remember that when certain verbs and prepositions are combined, they sometimes have special meanings.

Column A	Column B
_____ 1. give up	a. discover
_____ 2. find out	b. do something finally
_____ 3. ask out	c. trust
_____ 4. pay for	d. make final payment
_____ 5. believe in	e. stop trying
_____ 6. pay off	f. invite
_____ 7. end up	g. buy

▶ Compare your answers with a partner. Try to agree on the same answers.

€xpanding Your Language

Speaking

▶ **Role Play: Interviewing** Prepare an interview like the one you read in this chapter. You can choose the same topic or one that is similar, such as marriage. Work with a partner or in a small group. Decide on the roles you will act out. Include the role of the interviewer. Prepare a list of questions for the interviewer to ask. Prepare the answers that your characters will give. Write out the script for the interview. Use your script to act out the interview, but do not memorize the lines. Be creative.

Writing

▶ **Interview** Talk to three people about a date they have gone on. Complete the following chart to prepare notes to write from.

	Where did you go?	What did you do?	Was it interesting or not?	Explain.
Name 1:				
Name 2:				
Name 3:				

▶ Use your notes to write about dating. You can include information comparing dating now to dating in the past or about dating in different countries. Write about an interesting date that you had or would like to go on.

Online Study Center   For additional activities, go to the *Reading Matters* Online Study Center at *college.hmco.com/pic/wholeyone2e.*

8 Learning to Live Together

▶ Chapter Openers

Discussion Questions

▶ **The Rules of Relationships** Think about these questions. Share your ideas with a partner or in a small group.

1. Who do you live with in your home?
2. What rules do people have to follow in your home?
3. How do you know if someone you are living with is happy or unhappy?
4. What do roommates need to know about each other before moving in together ?
5. a. Should people take marriage education courses before they get married?
   b. What would they learn about in these courses?

▶ Paired Readings

▶ In this section, you will find two different stories on the same theme. Choose one of the stories to read. Prepare to explain the text to someone who read the same story and then to a person who read the other story.

▶ These are two articles about people who are planning to share their living space—one couple that is planning to get married and two friends who plan to share an apartment. You will find out about the challenges they face. Work with a partner who is reading the same text.

① Preparing for a Roommate

Getting Information from Illustrations

▶ Work with your partner and take turns explaining what you see in the picture in the reading. Read the story title and answer the following question to predict what the story will be about.

In North America, when two people rent an apartment, they usually sign a lease. Do both people need to sign?

_____

**Understanding
the Main Idea**

▶ Read the story, then check your prediction. Correct it if necessary.

What is the main idea of the story?

_____

**Understanding
Details**

▶ Answer the questions after each paragraph. In the story, underline the facts that support your answer. Write the question number in the margin of the reading.

Writing "The Roommate Rules"

❶　　Jamie and Kathy met in college. They became good friends. They liked the same things: chocolate fudge ice cream, live jazz bands, and action movies without much of a story to them. They even took vacations together. They were very close friends and shared a lot. They went to the same yoga class, read the same books, and had a lot of friends in common. They were always there for each other. Then, in the last year of college, Jamie and Kathy decided to get an apartment together. Jamie found a great apartment and was very excited that Kathy liked it very much too. They were ready to sign the lease the next day. Then, Jamie's brother had a suggestion—they should make a written agreement before signing the lease.

---

1. Where did Jamie and Kathy meet?

_____

2. How did they become friends?

_____

3. How close did they become?

_____

4. What did they decide to do in their last year of college?

_____

5. What suggestion did Jamie's brother have for them?

_____

❷   At first, Jamie was surprised at her brother's suggestion. She imagined that sharing an apartment would be easy for them because they were such good friends. But his advice was to sign a document that spelled out the rules they would both live by. What were the rules he had in mind? Some basic points included signing the lease in both names, agreeing to pay the rent on time, and agreeing to divide all the bills, such as cable, telephone, electricity, and groceries, equally. Other rules could include sharing responsibility for cooking and cleaning. There could even be a rule about whether or not to have friends stay in the apartment and for how long.

1. How did Jamie react to her brother's suggestion?

_____

2. Why did Jamie think sharing an apartment would be easy?

_____

3. What kind of agreement did Jamie's brother suggest?

_____

4. What basic points would the agreement include?

_____

5. What other rules could be included?

_____

❸   Are these agreements really necessary? To find out, Jamie talked to a classmate who told her that he and his friend wrote an agreement before they became roommates. They agreed to rules about how late to have friends over, how loud to play music, how often to clean up in the kitchen, and how to share the common living spaces such as bathrooms and living rooms. They look at their agreement every time they have a disagreement. They check the agreement and then decide how to handle the problem. They compromise or change things as they go along. Jamie and Kathy agreed that sharing an apartment means sharing responsibility. They knew that it's easy for little arguments to grow and become major battles. To avoid battles, it's better to have the rules on paper. Jamie and Kathy talked it over and decided to make a written agreement they called "The Roommate Rules." Together they wrote an agreement they hope will help them stay friends as well as roommates.

1. What did Jamie want to learn from her classmate?

   _____

2. What rules did the classmate and his roommate agree to before they lived together?

   _____

3. When do they look at their agreement?

   _____

4. What did Jamie and Kathy agree to do?

   _____

5. Why did they make this decision?

   _____

▶ Work with a partner. Take turns reading the questions and answers. Refer to the reading if your answers are different.

Recapping the Story

▶ Reread the first paragraph quickly. Cover the information and tell your partner as much as you can remember. Ask for help if you forget or give incorrect information. Take turns reading and retelling the information in all of the paragraphs.

Reacting to the Story

▶ Discuss these questions with a partner.

1. What do you think of making a written agreement before moving in with a friend? Explain what you would do in a similar situation. Give the reasons for your opinion.

2. What would you tell a friend to include in an agreement like "The Roommate Rules?"

❷Preparing for Marriage

Getting Information from Illustrations

▶ Work with your partner and take turns explaining what you see in the picture in the reading. Read the story title and answer the following question to predict what the story will be about.

What kind of preparations do couples need to make before they get married?

_____

Understanding the Main Idea

▶ Read the story, then check your prediction. Correct it, if necessary.

What is the main idea of this story?

_____

Understanding Details

▶ Answer the questions after each paragraph. In the story, underline the facts that support your answer. Write the question number in the margin of the reading.

What's Your Marriage IQ?

❶   Judy and Dave love each other. They began dating four years ago and now they plan to get married. They think that they are ready for marriage. After all, they both have well-paying management jobs so they have saved some money. They like the same things—they both enjoy camping out, going to rock concerts, driving motorcycles, and going out for Japanese food. They both know and enjoy each other's families and friends. Judy was ready to start making their wedding plans. Then, Judy's sister had a suggestion—they should go to a marriage education course first.

1. How do Judy and Dave feel about each other?

   _____

2. What makes them think they're ready for marriage?

   _____

3. What was Judy beginning to do?

   _____

4. What suggestion did Judy's sister have?

   _____

---

❷   Judy was surprised at her sister's suggestion and she wasn't sure how to respond. After four years of dating, she thought that she and Dave knew each other and that they were ready for marriage. But her sister's advice made her think. Married couples sometimes run into problems that they didn't think of before the wedding. As part of the marriage education course, couples learn some very basic but important questions to think about. Do they know about each other's finances? Do they agree about how they want to spend their hard-earned money? How important is it to have a budget and keep to it? What kind of home do they want to have in the future? Do they hope to have children right away, later, or at all? If one of them had a good job offer in another part of the country, would the other person move? Or would they decide to live in different cities?

---

1. How did Judy react to her sister's suggestion?

   _____

2. Why did Judy think she was ready for marriage?

   _____

3. What did her sister's advice make her think about?

   _____

4. Name three basic subjects couples would think about in the marriage course.

   _____

❸   Judy and Dave decided to take a marriage education course. At first they didn't think they would like it. But now they are very enthusiastic. They look forward to every class. They love the practical information and the useful advice they are getting. Dave says, "We get in the car afterwards and we start talking right away. The conversation just keeps on going even after we get home. These classes bring up so many things I wouldn't have thought of. After all, I realize that we have two distinctly different personalities and we have to take the time to understand each other if we want our marriage to work." Judy says, "I'm an optimist, so I never had any doubts that being married to Dave would be good. I never really looked ahead and imagined the possible problems that we'd have to work out. But now, after this course, I'm a realist too. I really understand that all marriages take communication as well as love for them to work."

1. What did Judy and Dave decide to do?

   _____

2. How did they feel about this at first?

   _____

3. How and why did their opinion change?

   _____

4. What does Dave like about driving home after the class?

   _____

5. What important things did Dave learn in these classes?

   _____

6. What does Judy now understand because of these classes?

   _____

▶ Work with a partner. Take turns reading the questions and answers. Refer to the reading if you have different answers.

Recapping the Story

▶ Reread the first paragraph quickly. Then cover the information and tell your partner as much as you can remember. Ask for help if you forget or give incorrect information. Take turns reading and retelling the information in all of the paragraphs.

Reacting to the Story

▶ Discuss these questions with a partner.

1. What do you think of taking marriage education classes? Do you think they are necessary? Give reasons for your opinion.

2. Who should teach a marriage education course? What would people need to do to "pass" the course?

Comparing the Readings

Discussing the Stories

▶ **A** Work with a partner who read a different story. Together, complete the following chart.

Questions	Jamie and Kathy	Judy and Dave
1. What are they planning to do?		
2. Who made an unusual suggestion to them?		
3. What was their first reaction?		
4. How did their first reaction change?		
5. Why did their first reaction change?		
6. What did they decide to do in the end?		

▶ From the information in the chart, circle the things that the people in these stories have in common. Prepare to explain what is similar in the two stories.

▶ **B** Discuss the questions in the "Reacting to the Story" section for both readings. In addition, decide what you think about the following questions.

1. Is it easy to have a good relationship with a roommate? Why or why not?

2. Is it easy to have a good relationship with a wife/husband? Why or why not?

3. What advice would you give to a friend who is planning to move in with a roommate?

4. What advice would you give to a friend who is planning to get married?

5. What do you think of television shows about finding the "right" man or woman? Why are they popular?

❯Vocabulary Building

Word Form and Meaning

▶ **A** Match the words in Column A with their meanings in Column B.

Column A

_____ 1. agree

_____ 2. finance

_____ 3. realize

_____ 4. respond

_____ 5. understand

Column B

a. to know something

b. to become aware of something new

c. to pay for something

d. to have the same opinion or idea

e. to answer to something or someone

▶ **B** Study these five words in their various forms: verb, noun, adjective, and adverb. The forms are not in the same order in each column. Choose the correct form to fill out the chart below. These words are commonly found in general and academic texts.

agree (v.)	finance (v.)	realize (v.)	respond (v.)	understand (v.)
agreement (n.)	finance	realized	response	understanding
agreed (adj.)	financing	realizing	responsively	understandable
agreeing (adj.)	financed	realizable	responding	understandably
agreeable (adj.)	financial	realization	responsive	understanding
agreeably (adv.)	financier			
	financially			

Verb	Noun	Adjective	Adverb
finance	1.	1.	1.
	2.	2.	
		3.	
realize	1.	1.	
		2.	
		3.	
respond	1.	1.	1.
		2.	
understand	1.	1.	1.
		2.	

▶ Compare lists with a partner. Try to agree on the same answers.

▶ **C** Write three sentences using words from the list.

▶ **D** Many words have more than one form. Look at the different forms and meanings for the word *finance*.

a. **finance (noun):** The study of the system of money
b. **finances (noun):** The money and other resources of a person or institution
c. **finance (verb):** To provide the money needed for a project

▶ Read the sentences below and write the letter of the correct form on the line provided.

1. _____ She was able to convince the couple that they should **finance** their daughter's education.

2. _____ She was able to convince the couple that they had the necessary **finances** to afford the rent.

3. _____ Does she want to finish her degree in **finance** next year?

4. _____ Can you make the necessary arrangements to **finance** the car?

5. _____ Did you have trouble agreeing on the **finances** for the coming year?

Vocabulary in Context

▶ **A** Complete each sentence with one of the adjectives from the following list. Use the words in boldface to help you choose your answer.

a. written   b. useful   c. well-paying   d. excited
e. hard-earned   f. possible   g. common

1. Jamie found a great apartment and was very _____ that Kathy **liked it very much** too.

2. I hadn't **looked ahead** and really imagined the _____ problems that we'd have to work out.

3. They had to decide **how to share** the _____ living spaces like bathrooms and living rooms.

4. **After working for so many years**, they discovered they couldn't agree on how to spend their _____ money.

5. They should make a _____ agreement before **signing** the lease.

6. They love the **practical** information and the _____ advice they are getting.

7. They both have _____ management jobs so they have **saved some money**.

▶ Compare your answers with a partner. Take turns reading your sentences.

▶ **B Antonyms** Match the word or phrase in Column A with its antonym in Column B.

Column A

_____ 1. married

_____ 2. look forward

_____ 3. different

_____ 4. doubting

_____ 5. dreamer

_____ 6. usual

_____ 7. unwritten

_____ 8. agreement

_____ 9. optimist

Column B

a. unusual

b. written

c. look back

d. pessimist

e. disagreement

f. decided

g. similar

h. unmarried

i. realist

▶ Compare your answers with a partner.

▶ **C** We add the prefixes *un-*, *dis-*, or *in-* to make a word that means the opposite. Find three examples from the list above. Write three sentences with these words. Reread the texts and look for other words that can begin with a negative prefix. Use a thesaurus or dictionary to help you find the words that have an opposite meaning.

▶ **D Categorizing** In each of these groups, circle the word that does not belong. Prepare to explain the reason for your choice.

1. cable   electricity   telephone   rent   cooking

2. married   independent   divorced   single   widowed

3. girlfriend   roommate   classmate   father   boyfriend

4. lease   kitchen   bathroom   living room   bedroom

5. understand   imagine   decide   think   communicate

▶ **Pair Work** Tell your answer and the reason it doesn't belong.

❯Expanding Your Language

Reading

This reading expands on the idea of relationships. There are many different marriage traditions that people follow. One of these is arranged marriages. In arranged marriages, a person who is a matchmaker arranges for the woman and man to meet each other. A matchmaker is usually a family member and the man and woman do not usually know each other. Notice how much easier it is to understand this now that you have already done some reading on this topic.

▶ Before beginning, read the following questions. After reading, answer them based on the information in the text.

1. Who is Sam Telap?
2. What is his life like?
3. What did he do when he decided to get married and why?
4. What are some of the ways that people who want to marry can use to meet each other?
5. What different methods of meeting people did Sam use?
6. Which methods were successful; which ones were not?
7. What is Sam planning to do?
8. What advice did Sam's mother give him?

Sam Telap's Wedding

Sam Telap is a twenty-nine-year-old accountant with a great education and good corporate job. He loves popular music and the latest movies. He feels right at home in New York—with a great apartment and an exciting Western lifestyle. But when it came to marriage, Sam decided to follow a tradition from his native India. He called his family and asked them to help find a bride for him.

Nowadays there are many ways to arrange an introduction for someone who wants to get married. Family introductions, newspaper ads, and websites provide opportunities to meet the right person. For Telap, he first tried a family-style introduction. His grandmother set him up with the granddaughter of a friend attending her temple. "It didn't go well," he said of the blind date. Then, he asked his uncle to run an ad in the ten-page matrimonial section of a major newspaper in India. The ad read: "Hindu boy, 29, chartered accountant, U.S.-born and residing, seeks intelligent, attractive, professional Hindu girl, 24–27." The last line included his e-mail address.

He received more than ninety responses; five came from North America, five from Africa, ten from Europe, and more than seventy came from India. With his parents' help, he made a choice of twenty-five potential brides. This summer he will travel to India to meet most of them, but says he already has one particular woman in mind. His parents spoke to an MBA in marketing and he'd like to meet her this summer. What about romantic love? Sam says, "I trust my mother's advice. She says you start to love the person after a while. It's worked for millions, so I have no doubt it will work for me."

Speaking

A Role Play Work with a partner. Choose the role of one of the people in these stories, such as Judy, her sister, or Dave, or Jamie, her brother, or Kathy. Together, write out the conversation between two people, based on the story and on ideas of your own.

Here is one example of how to begin the conversation:

Judy: Hi sis, do you have a minute? I want you to look at my wedding plans.
Sister: Sure. I have time, but look at this ad for a course for people planning to marry. What do you think of it?

B Two-Minute Taped Talk Record a two-minute audiotape or audio CD about one of the stories in this chapter. To make your recording, follow the steps on pages 65–66.

Writing

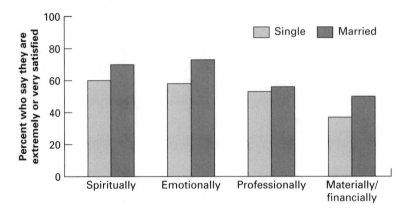

❿ **A** **Writing Sentences from Information in a Graph**   Look at the following graph and use the information to write sentences of your own about married or single Americans.

Example: Fifty percent of *married* Americans say that they are very satisfied with their lives financially. Thirty-seven percent of *single* Americans say that they are very satisfied with their lives financially. Thirteen percent more *married* Americans are very satisfied with their lives financially than are *single* Americans.

❿ **B** **Personal Writing**   Based on the ideas you discussed in this chapter, as well as any ideas of your own, write ten to fifteen sentences about one of the following:

1. Your thoughts and feelings about the kinds of relationships you read about
2. The kinds of relationships that you had or would have in the future
3. The life of a single person compared to the life of a married person

Online Study Center   For additional activities, go to the *Reading Matters* Online Study Center at *www.college.hmco.com/pic/wholeyone2e*.

9 Neighbors

Chapter Openers

Matching

▷ **A** Match the word in Column A with its definition in Column B.

Column A

_____ 1. neighbors

_____ 2. neighborhood

Column B

a. an area where people live and that has its own special identity

b. people who live near or next to one another

▷ Work with a partner to discuss your answers.

▷ **B** Think of some examples of neighborhoods that you have lived in or have heard about. Describe what they are like.

Agree or Disagree?

▷ Read the following statements. Write *A* if you agree or *D* if you disagree. Give the reasons for your choices.

_____ 1. People who live in a neighborhood usually know one another.

_____ 2. You can call a neighbor for help if you are feeling sick or need to go to the hospital.

_____ 3. Neighbors don't talk to one another very often.

_____ 4. You can call your neighbor to help if you have problems with your heat, water, or electricity.

_____ 5. Neighbors get together for fun activities, such as street parties or barbecues.

_____ 6. People can ask their neighbors when they need to borrow ordinary things, such as chairs and tables, or food, such as sugar or milk.

_____ 7. Neighbors often help one another to look after their children.

▷ Discuss your answers with others in a small group.

Exploring and Understanding Reading

Previewing

▶ To preview, read the title and the first and last sentences of each paragraph in the reading. Based on that information, check (✔) the ideas you expect to find out about from the following list.

1. _____ The stories of people who are good neighbors

2. _____ How to make your neighborhood safe from crime

3. _____ Different ways neighbors help one another

4. _____ The difficulties of meeting your neighbors

5. _____ The reasons people get to know their neighbors

6. _____ Stories of people who fall in love with their neighbors

▶ Compare your choices with a partner. Try to agree on your answers. Then read all of the paragraphs. See whether you should change any of the choices you made.

In the Neighborhood: Modern Success Stories

❶   In this neighborhood, there are a number of people who are in need of a little help. Cynthia Marks is a single mother who finds it difficult to work at her job as an office administrator all day and to put dinner on the table every night for her four kids. "Usually, I'm so tired at the end

of the day that I bring home pizza for them to eat." Cynthia decided that she had to do something. She didn't want to spend her food budget on expensive take-out food. Also, she wanted her kids to have a well-balanced, nutritious meal. She talked to her neighbor, Ann Cullen, another single mother with two children, who works full time as a legal secretary. Ann understood Cynthia's needs. She, too, often felt impatient and angry having to coordinate the cooking and cleaning after working all day. She didn't want to be angry, and she wanted to spend more time with her kids at home. So the two neighbors thought of a plan. They decided that they would take turns cooking for each other's families once a week. They were ready for a change. They had a feeling that this would improve their lives.

❷   There are hundreds of neighborhoods in which people need some help to do ordinary chores. Neighborhood groups exist to help people in a number of different ways. There are groups that take older people who can no longer drive or take public transportation to do their grocery shopping or make other purchases on their own. These senior citizens really appreciate being able to have some independence in their lives. There are neighborhood crime-watch groups that keep an eye on people's homes and watch for any signs of robberies or other crimes. There are child-safety programs that ask adults to watch out for neighborhood children who may need to come to a safe home in an emergency.

❸   Cynthia and Ann's plan was a success. They now share meal making and sometimes eat together with three other neighbors. According to Ann, cooking for a group once a week is better than cooking five nights a week for three. In addition to sharing dinner, Cynthia and Ann get to talk about their problems and responsibilities. They find it is beneficial just to be able to discuss a problem with another adult. With their neighbors, they discuss the neighborhood school their young children attend and let each other know about special sales in neighborhood stores or social events that will be taking place. According to these women, they were able to build a relationship that has improved their lives.

Note Taking

Key words are the words that are important to understanding the ideas. Look at the key words in boldface in this sentence: She **brought** the **children** their **dinner**. Usually, the nouns and verbs in a sentence are key words. Questions after a reading help you find the key words you need to underline. ▪

▶ **A Finding the Key Words** Answer these questions in notes. When you write notes, remember to write only the key words, not the whole sentence. In the story, underline the key words and write the question numbers in the margin near the line where you found the information.

1. What is some personal information about Cynthia and Ann?

	Cynthia	Ann
a. Marital status:		
b. Employment:		
c. Children:		

2. What problems do Cynthia and Ann have?

	Cynthia	Ann
a. Problem:		
b. Feelings:		
c. Didn't want:		
d. Wanted:		
e. Solution:		

3. According to the reading, what are some ways that neighborhood groups can help people?

	People and Problems	Help that Some People Can Offer
a.		
b.		
c.		

4. What do Cynthia, Ann, and their neighbors talk about when they meet for dinner?

a. _____

b. _____

▶ Work with a partner. Take turns answering the questions. Refer to the story if you have different information.

▶ **B** Circle *T* for true and *F* for false. Use the information from your notes if you are not sure of the answer. If the statement is false, give the correct information.

1. T F   Cynthia and Ann are both single mothers.

2. T F   Cynthia and Ann both have four children.

3. T F   Cynthia feels angry and impatient at night.

4. T F   Cynthia and Ann decided to take turns cooking for each other's families twice a week.

5. T F   There are a number of neighborhood groups that help others.

6. T F   Older people can always drive or take public transportation to do their shopping.

7. T F   Crime-watch groups watch their neighbors' homes.

8. T F   There are no safe homes for children in the neighborhood.

9. T F   Cynthia and Ann now cook for a group of people every night.

10. T F   Cynthia and Ann like to talk about their problems at dinner.

▶ Work with a partner. Take turns answering the questions. Refer to the reading in cases where you disagree.

Reacting to the Reading

▶ Discuss these questions with a partner or others in a small group.

1. What do Cynthia and Ann enjoy about being neighbors?

2. When do neighbors get to meet one another in your neighborhood? For example, would you meet your neighbors at church, at the store, at the gym, or at a meeting?

3. Is it more difficult for neighbors to get to know one another in other countries than in the United States? Why or why not?

4. What is your neighborhood like? Describe the people and places that you know.

5. What makes a neighborhood attractive or interesting to people? What makes it uninteresting or unattractive to people?

6. Do you enjoy cooking or eating in a group? Why or why not?

❽Vocabulary Building

Word Form and Meaning

▶ **A** Match the words in Column A with their meanings in Column B.

Column A

_____ 1. administrate

_____ 2. appreciate

_____ 3. benefit

_____ 4. discuss

_____ 5. purchase

Column B

a. to talk with someone

b. to buy something

c. to be responsible for carrying out a plan or a program

d. to gain something from an experience or a person

e. to realize the good of or be thankful for something

▶ **B** Study these five words in their various forms: verb, noun, adjective, and adverb. The forms are not in the same order in each column. Then choose the correct form to fill out the chart on the next page. These words are commonly found in general and academic texts.

administrate (v.)	appreciate (v.)	benefit (v.)	discuss (v.)	purchase (v.)
administrator (n.)	appreciative	beneficiary	discussion	purchase
administration (n.)	appreciated	beneficially	discussed	purchased
administrative (adj.)	appreciation	benefit	discussing	purchaser
administrated (adj.)	appreciatively	beneficial	discussion	purchasing
administratively (adv.)		benefit		

Verb	Noun	Adjective	Adverb
appreciate	1.	1.	1.
		2.	
benefit	1.	1.	1.
	2.	2.	
discuss	1.	1.	
		2.	
		3.	
purchase	1.	1.	
	2.	2.	

▶ Compare lists with a partner. Try to agree on the same answers.

▶ **C** Write three sentences using words from the list.

▶ **D Verbs: Present and Past** Write the past form of the following verbs. Circle these past tense verbs in the reading.

1. decide   _____

2. want   _____

3. talk   _____

4. understand   _____

5. feel   _____

6. think   _____

7. is   _____

8. have   _____

▶ Compare your answers with a partner. Write three sentences and three questions of your own, using both the present and past forms of any of these verbs.

Vocabulary in Context

▶ **A** Complete each sentence with one of the words from the following list. Decide whether you need a noun, an adjective, or a verb in the sentence. Look for clues in the sentence to help you understand the meaning. In the sentence, underline the words that helped you to choose your answer.

a. attend	b. chores	c. discuss
d. ordinary	e. responsibilities	f. spend

1. The neighborhood looks very _____, but the relationships that people have there are very special.

2. She has so many different _____ that she doesn't have enough time to relax.

3. They felt very tired and didn't want to finish the household _____, such as the laundry and the shopping.

4. How much time to you need to _____ on making dinner?

5. Did you _____ the meeting last week? I don't remember seeing you.

6. I need to _____ this problem with you. When can we meet to talk?

▶ Compare your answers with a partner. Take turns reading the statements.

▶ **B** Circle *N* if the word in boldface is a noun, or *V* if it is a verb. Then write a sentence using the word as a different part of speech.

1. N V   She has a lot of different **needs** that are difficult to meet.

2. N V   Her **work** is very important to her.

3. N V   Can I **help** you to carry in those packages?

4. N V   She decided to **share** her sandwich with him because she wasn't very hungry.

5. N V   Can you **budget** enough money for us to pay for new equipment?

6. N V   Will the disk **drive** work on this computer?

7. N V   If they **sign** the card today, we can send it in the mail.

▶ Compare your answers with a partner.

C Prepositions Complete these sentences with the correct preposition from the following list.

   a. in   b. for   c. of   d. with   e. to   f. on

1. They decided to try cooking _____ each other.

2. She helped him in a number _____ different ways.

3. She lived _____ this neighborhood _____ many years.

4. They worked together _____ three other women.

5. According _____ the experts, this program will help you.

6. Your neighbors will keep an eye _____ your house during the day.

In the reading, find three sentences with prepositions. Circle the preposition and the word or words that go with it. Compare your answers with a partner. Take turns reading the sentences.

Expanding Your Language

Reading

This reading expands on the idea of neighbors. There are many different housing communities all over the world. One of these is a co-housing community. In co-housing communities, people choose to live close to other people and share some of the housing. It is an unusual kind of community for many reasons. Notice how much easier it is to understand this now that you have already done some reading on this topic.

Before beginning, read the following questions. After reading, answer them based on the information in the text.

1. Where is co-housing popular?
2. What two ideas does it combine?
3. Who designs and manages a co-housing community?
4. What part of the community is private and what is shared?
5. What is the commons and why is it important?
6. What purposes does the common house serve?
7. Who lives in co-housing communities?
8. What are the advantages of living in a co-housing community?

Co-Housing: A Model for the Suburbs

Co-housing began in Europe in the 1970s. It combined two ideas: the idea of the home as a private place and the idea of home within a community. The idea quickly spread to the United States, where there are now over 140 co-housing projects planned.

What is a co-housing community?

A co-housing community is designed and then managed by the residents themselves. In a typical co-housing community, there are thirty or so small houses. Residents own or rent their own living space. These individual houses are built around a green commons area and a common house that serves as a community gathering place.

What is the commons?

The commons is a place for playing, visiting with neighbors, or just lounging in the sun. The design of the entire community allows people to live in a much smaller area without feeling crowded and without taking over too much valuable farmland, forest, grassland and wildlife habitat.

What is the common house?

The heart of a co-housing community is the common house. The common house is shared among all the people in the community. It is a gathering place for meetings or just getting together with friends. The common house typically contains a large community kitchen and eating area for meals prepared by community members one to three times a week. In the common house, there is enough room for large dinner parties or for family gatherings. Most common houses have laundry facilities, exercise rooms, and rooms for people who are visiting to sleep. Some common houses have community office space. People who work at home can share office equipment such as fax and copy machines. Students can get together to study their homework. The common house also has a community workshop. People can use the tools in the workshop. People save money by buying tools for everyone to use. Many communities have their own gardens. They grow food for their families and share the food with other people in the community.

Who lives in a co-housing community?

Co-housing is a wonderful place for people of different ages to live. There are young families who live there. The community has a child-care center in the common house, so parents can work without worrying about their children. There are families and couples of all ages who live there. And it is a great place for adults. Residents often go for a walk in the evening and stop to visit their neighbors. There are old people who live there also. The co-housing community is a good place to grow old. There is always someone around to offer help.

Speaking

▶ **Talk It Out** Think about the topic of neighbors. Make a list of the benefits of knowing your neighbors and then a list of the problems with neighbors. Look at the sample ideas and add three ideas of your own.

Benefits of Knowing Your Neighbors	Problems with Neighbors
• I can call if I need a ride to school.	Loud music bothers me at night.
• I can borrow milk if I run out of it.	They often argue with me.
• _____	_____
• _____	_____
• _____	_____

▶ Work with a partner and compare your lists. Discuss your own experiences with neighbors.

Writing

▶ **A Personal Reactions** Look closely at the neighborhood you live in now. Compare that neighborhood to another neighborhood, such as the one where you grew up. Write about both places, and compare the people and places of both neighborhoods. Work with a partner and describe the neighborhoods you wrote about.

▶ **B** Is a co-housing community described in the reading your idea of an ideal community? What is your idea of an ideal neighborhood? Write about what you think an ideal neighborhood should include.

▶ Read On: Taking It Further

Reading Cloze

▶ Use the words from the unit listed here to fill in the blanks in this paragraph.

a. date (2×)	b. describe (2×)	c. find	d. give	e. have
f. meet	g. number	h. old	i. popular	j. put	k. tall

How do people meet others they would like to date? One way is to

(1) _____ an ad in the personals section of the newspaper.

Advertising for a (2) _____ is not a new idea; it is almost as

(3) _____ as newspapers are. Putting an advertisement in the

personals is still (4) _____ today. But many people say that this

is not the way to find a date. What are the problems? One man said that his

(5) _____ didn't look like the description she gave. She didn't

(6) _____ blond hair and wasn't (7) _____ and thin.

Another problem is that it's difficult to (8) _____ yourself in an ad.

Most ads are about 100 words. It's difficult to (9) _____ yourself in

100 words. But even if you don't (10) _____ anyone interesting,

personals give you a chance to introduce yourself to someone new. But

remember this advice: Be sure to (11) _____ in a public place, such

as a coffee shop or a bar. And never (12) _____ your home address or

phone (13) _____.

▶ Compare your answers with a partner.

Newspaper Articles

 Reading Tip

Don't forget to write in your **reading journal** and to enter new words for this chapter in your **vocabulary log**. Show your journal and log entries to your teacher. ■

▶ Check the newspaper for articles about neighborhoods, living arrangements, marriages, or other relationships you read about in this unit. Ask your teacher for short articles that you can read. One suggestion is to look for articles about relationships in an advice column in the newspaper. Another is to find an article in the Living or Home section of the weekend newspaper. Read the article over until you have a good idea of the important facts of the story. Explain your article to a partner or in a small group.

*Online Study Center*

For additional activities, go to the *Reading Matters* Online Study Center at *college.hmco.com/pic/wholeyone2e*.

The Challenge of Sports Today

The first thing is
to love your sport.
Never do it to
please someone
else. It has to be
yours.

—*Peggy Fleming*

Introducing the Topic

Sports today are both very difficult and very exciting. In this unit, you will find out about a variety of sports that appeal to various types of people. Chapter 10 is about competing in an interesting sport, the triathlon, and the development of this recent sport. Chapter 11 compares the thrills of outdoor and indoor sports events. Chapter 12 takes a look at the types of preparations that today's Olympic athletes make.

▶Points of Interest

What kinds of challenges do you think this person faced?

The Challenge of the Triathlon

Chapter Openers

Getting Information from Illustrations

A Under each picture, write the letter of the statement that it best matches.

1. _____ 2. _____

3. _____ 4. _____

a. Triathletes are very dedicated people. They spend hours training before a competition.
b. After they finish swimming, triathletes compete in a long bicycle race.
c. Triathletes finish the event with a marathon distance run.
d. The triathlon begins with a swimming race.

▶ **B** What do you know about the triathlon? Describe what people do in the triathlon: what they need in order to compete, where they train and compete, and why they like the triathlon event. Give your opinion of the triathlon: Is it difficult or not?

Discussion Questions

▶ **Practicing Sports** Think about these questions. Discuss your ideas with a partner or in a small group.

1. What are some sports you like to practice? Give the reasons you like the sport.
2. What are some sports you like to watch?
3. What is enjoyable or difficult about each of these sports:
   a. bicycling
   b. swimming
   c. running
4. What do athletes have to do to prepare for sports competitions? What is the reason that people devote time to preparing for competitions?

▶Exploring and Understanding Reading

Predicting

▶ Circle *T* for true or *F* for false.

1. T F The triathlon has three events in one competition.
2. T F It takes 24 hours to complete a triathlon.
3. T F It takes many years of training to prepare for a triathlon race.
4. T F The triathlon is a very old sports event.
5. T F Only top athletes in their twenties compete in triathlons.
6. T F The triathlon is an Olympic sport.

> **Reading Tip**

To read quickly, **look at groups of two or three words together**. Don't read one word at a time. Continue reading through the information until you reach the end. Then return to the start of the article to reread. ■

▶ Quickly read the following selection. Review your answers after you finish the reading. Make any changes necessary. If the statement is false, give the correct information.

Getting Ready for the "Ironman"

❶   The triathlon is a demanding sport. Many say that it is a real test of an athlete's body and mind. It is difficult because it is three sports in one. It includes swimming for 2.4 miles (3.84 kilometers), bicycling for 112 miles (180 kilometers), and running for 26.2 miles (41.9 kilometers). It takes a lot of strength and willpower to compete. The top triathletes finish all three events in about 8 hours. This sport is a real challenge. First, it takes time and stamina to train for competitions. Some people spend up to 8 months training for the race. The training demands a lot of physical energy and strength. During training, the athletes will bike 320 km, swim 10 km, and run 56 km every week. Second, it takes money to compete. The equipment is not cheap. Bicycles for this event can cost up to $10,000. Top-quality swimming gear and running shoes are expensive. Athletes have to pay to enter the race. Some individuals estimate that they spend more than half of their incomes on training. Third, athletes must have strong minds. It takes willpower to push themselves to keep training to reach their goal.

❷   The triathlon is a recent sport. Triathlons began in California in the early 1970s. There, some athletes started the three-sport race because they wanted to make their training exciting. One of these athletes moved to Hawaii and took the sport with him. In 1978, competitors held the first professional triathlon race in Hawaii. It was called the Ironman World Championship. In 1982, this race became famous because of the televised performance of Julie Moss. She was twenty-three years old, and it was her first competition. Exhausted, she was running toward the finish line. Suddenly, 3 meters before the line, she fell down. She tried to get up, but she kept falling. She finally crawled across the finish line. Television cameras showed the world her dramatic struggle. She lost that year, but she tried again. Finally, in 1985, she won Ironman Japan. This was the start of the Ironman's popularity.

❸   Today, triathlons are much more popular among ordinary athletes. People of all ages—from teens to seventies—can compete, as long as they are in good physical condition. In fact, it has become a great family sport, with fathers and mothers training with their sons and daughters. Triathletes are special people who have time in their lives for careers and families. Most are highly educated and earn top salaries in their jobs. They are people who are intensely competitive. Many triathletes are happily married. In fact, two-thirds of triathletes say that their training has a positive influence on their marriages. Today, the triathlon is an Olympic sport and a respected event worldwide.

Understanding the Main Ideas

▶ Write the number of the paragraph that best fits each of these main ideas.

a. _____ Today, the triathlon is a sport that many people can train to compete in.

b. _____ Triathlon competitions are a new development in the history of sport.

c. _____ A triathlete has to be very strong in many different ways to practice this sport.

Understanding Details

▶ Answer the following questions. Underline the words in the reading that support your answer. Write the question number in the margin.

1. What sports does the triathlon combine?

_____

2. Why do people say that the triathlon is a demanding sport?

_____

3. What do people have to do to train for this sport?

_____

4. Why do people need money to compete?

_____

5. a. How did the sport of triathlon begin?

_____

   b. How did the Ironman become famous?

_____

   c. How did it gain in popularity?

_____

6. a. What happened to Julie Moss in her triathlon of 1982?

_____

   b. What happened in her triathlon of 1985?

_____

7. Why are triathlons becoming more popular?

_____

8. What are two qualities of people who like to compete in this sport?

_____

9. What two facts show how popular triathlons have become?

_____

▶ Compare your answers with a partner. Take turns reading your answers. Refer to the reading in cases where you disagree.

Note Taking   ▶ Find the information to complete this chart from the reading. Write the details in note form, as shown in the example below.

Sport	Swimming	Biking	Running
Distance	2.4 miles (3.84 km)		
Training			
Cost			expensive

▶ Work with a partner to compare your information. Write two questions about the information. For example, you could ask, "Which sport covers the longest distance?"

1. _____

2. _____

Applying the Information

▶ **Problem Solving** Use the information from the reading and your own experience to complete this activity. Read the following stories and decide whom to pick for a triathlon team. Put the candidates in order from best (1) to last (3). Be sure to have the reasons for your choice.

A. Jed Allen is fifty years old. He is a single father with two teenage children. He likes to swim with his son and to bicycle with his daughter. He trains with them three days a week. When he was a university student, he won medals in marathon running. He is the president of a large clothing company. He would like to join the team. He thinks that his children would enjoy training with him as he prepares.

B. Jerry Fox is twenty years old. He is a medical student and wins honors in his university program. Jerry loves swimming and biking. He gets up at 6:00 every day and works out in the gym for two hours before school. Jerry's girlfriend is a triathlete. He wants to join the team so that they can train together.

C. Marian Lowe is forty years old. She is a mother and wife. She and her husband have a successful computer business. Marian is a champion swimmer and was a member of a national swim team. She likes a challenge and spends her weekends bicycling with her family. She runs with a group of friends. They started to do triatlon training two years ago. She is the best in her club.

▶ Work with a partner or in a small group and discuss your choices. Decide whom you will choose to join the team. Complete the following chart. Be prepared to explain why you think each person would be good on the team (pro) and why not (con).

Choice	Pros (Reasons for)	Cons (Reasons against)
1.		
2.		
3.		

◗Vocabulary Building

Word Form and Meaning

▶ **A** Match the words in Column A with their meanings in Column B.

Column A

_____ 1. compete

_____ 2. energize

_____ 3. equip

_____ 4. estimate

_____ 5. intensify

Column B

a. to guess the amount, size, or importance of something

b. to make something stronger or have something be stronger

c. to run against someone

d. to provide or supply someone with needed items

e. to give someone the power to continue

◗ B Study these five words in their various forms: verb, noun, adjective, and adverb. The forms are not in the same order in each column. Then choose the correct form to fill out the chart below. These words are commonly found in general and academic texts.

compete (v.)	energize (v.)	equip (v.)	estimate (v.)	intensify (v.)
competitor (n.)	energy	equipping	estimated	intensified
competition (n.)	energized	equipment	estimator	intense
competitive (adj.)	energizer	equipped	estimation	intensifying
competing (adj.)	energetically		estimating	intensification
competitively (adv.)	energetic			intensely

Verb	Noun	Adjective	Adverb
energize	1.	1.	1.
	2.	2.	
equip	1.	1.	
		2.	
estimate	1.	1.	
	2.	2.	
intensify	1.	1.	1.
		2.	
		3.	

◗ Compare lists with a partner. Try to agree on the same answers.

◗ C Write three sentences using words from the list.

◗ D In English, some nouns have an -ing ending. You will find examples of some of these kinds of nouns in the reading. Complete each of the following statements with the correct form of the word.

1. bicycle / bicycling

   I like _____ because it is such great exercise.

2. train / training

   You have to do a lot of _____ if you want to finish the race.

3. race / racing

Every month during her training, she would _____ in a 10 km competition.

4. swim / swimming

For me, _____ is the hardest part of the event.

5. run / running

He was so tired that he didn't think he would be able to _____ up the last hill.

▶ Compare your answers with a partner. Then take turns reading your sentences.

Vocabulary in Context

▶ **A** Complete each sentence with one of the words from the list. Underline the part of the sentence that helped you to choose your answer.

a. after	b. before	c. brought	d. equipment
e. finish	f. salary	g. test	h. tried

1. Top-quality _____, such as shoes and bicycles, is expensive.

2. The triathlon is a _____ that measures both the body and the mind.

3. She lost the first race, but she _____ again and won.

4. She tried to _____ the race, but she fell down before the end.

5. He _____ this sport to people in his new home.

6. She earned a good _____ in her new job.

7. She felt nervous _____ the race started but very good

_____ it was over.

▶ Compare your answers with a partner and take turns reading the completed sentences.

⏵ **B Antonyms** Match each word in Column A with its antonym in Column B.

Column A

Column B

_____ 1. finish

a. ordinary

_____ 2. expensive

b. cheap

_____ 3. run

c. crawl

_____ 4. get up

d. negative

_____ 5. lose

e. win

_____ 6. dramatic

f. fall down

_____ 7. positive

g. start

⏵ Use three of the pairs (the word and its opposite) above in sentences of your own.

1. _____

2. _____

3. _____

Expanding Your Language

Reading

The Ironman, the most famous triathlon race, takes place each year in Hawaii. Read about how the Ironman race began and the people who compete in this thrilling race, and find out what it involves. Notice how much easier it is to understand this now that you have already done some reading on this topic.

⏵ Before beginning, read the following questions. After reading, answer them based on the information in the text.

1. When did the Ironman race begin?
2. What was the purpose of the first race?
3. What did the race include?
4. How did the race become popular?
5. How many times has Dave Scott won?
6. What is the record for the winning time for men and for women?
7. Who won the Ironman in 2003?
8. How much prize money was given to the winners of the Ironman?
9. How many people competed in 2003?
10. Why is the race so popular?

The Ironman

The Ironman began as a triathlon competition on the island of Oahu, Hawaii, in February 1978. The purpose of the Ironman was to decide who was the fittest athlete in the sport. It combined a 2.4-mile open ocean swim, a 112-mile around-the-island bike race, and a 26.2-mile marathon. There were only fifteen participants in the first competition. But the magazine *Sports Illustrated* published an article about the Ironman in 1979. Many people read the article and some thought, "Wait a minute, I am a runner, a cyclist, and a swimmer. I keep a record of all my races, I check my weight, I train every day. I could do this too." Then in 1980, the TV network ABC decided to televise the event. It attracted a lot of attention—and a lot of participants who joined to compete. That year Dave Scott won the Ironman. He finished in nine hours, twenty-four minutes, and thirty-three seconds (9:24:33). It was almost two hours faster than the previous record, held by Tom Warren.

In 1981, the organizers moved the race from Oahu to Kona on the island of Hawaii, the Big Island. There the conditions were brutally hard. The water is rough and, on land, the dry hot winds make the bike and marathon courses almost impossible to complete. But there, in very difficult conditions, Dave Scott won six Ironmans in eight years. His best time was 8:10:13. That was almost an hour and a quarter faster than his first win. Twenty-five years later, the Ironman is still a popular race. In 2003, at the twenty-fifth anniversary race, there were 1,251 men and 397 women.

Over the years more than 500,000 people have completed the Ironman. The Ironman race celebrates those athletes who are able to endure. But it is a hard race. And it takes a lot of stamina, endurance, and the ability to survive. Mark Allen, who is married to triathlete Julie Moss, is a six-time triathlon winner and knows what it takes to compete. He won his first triathlon in a record 8:09:15. That record was lowered in 1996 to 8:04:08. The best time for women is 8:55:28, clocked by Paula Newby-Fraser in 1992. The 2003 race was won by Peter Reid, aged thirty-four, and Lori Bowden, aged thirty-six, of Canada. The husband and wife team were extremely happy with their results. Reid completed the competition in 8:22:35. Bowden took first place in the women's competition with a finishing time of 9:11:55. Each of the winners won US $100,000 in prize money. In all, $430,000 in prize money was given away.

The popularity of the Ironman race has grown and organizers expect that it will continue to attract serious athletes in the years to come. The athletes who compete are among the strongest and most dedicated of all.

Speaking

▶ **Oral Presentation** Choose a sport that is interesting to you or an athlete who is good at his or her sport. To prepare your presentation, follow these steps.

▶ **1.** Decide who or what you will present (the subject of your presentation). Find out whether the topic is interesting to your audience. Try to choose an unusual or little-known subject.

2. Read about the subject. To find information, check in the library for access to an online encyclopedia or ask your teacher.

3. Take notes of the information you want to present. Make an outline of these facts, as in the following example:

Subject of Presentation: Jackrabbit Johanson

Who he was:
- Canadian cross-country skier born in Norway

What he did:
- came to Quebec, Canada, in the 1950s
- lived with his family in a cabin north of Montreal
- lived in the woods; no electricity or running water
- made the first cross-country ski trail
- brought first group of skiers to the area

What he accomplished:
- made more than 100 km of trails for people to ski on
- made the sport popular in Canada
- taught many young people how to cross-country ski
- improved the practice of the sport
- led an annual 100 km race
- lived until 111 years old

Why I chose this topic:
- lived an unusual life; close to nature
- developed a sport that many people enjoy today
- lived a long, purposeful life

4. Practice your presentation. Write four questions for people to answer after your presentation.

Writing

▶ **A Personal Reactions** What is an athlete? What do you think about the sacrifices in time and training that people who are serious about a sport make? How can ordinary people participate in sports? Write your ideas about these questions.

▶ **B** Write a short paragraph about the topic you presented in your oral presentation. Use your notes to help you explain your ideas. Write as much information as you can. Give the paragraph to your teacher to read.

 **Online Study Center**

For additional activities, go to the **Reading Matters** Online Study Center at *college.hmco.com/pic/wholeyone2e.*

11 Looking for Excitement

Chapter Openers

Discussion
Questions

▶ **Thrilling Sports** Think about these questions. Discuss your ideas with a partner or in a small group.

1. What sports are popular to practice outdoors in the winter? What sports are popular to practice outdoors in the summer?
2. What sports are popular to practice in the city?
3. What are the differences between indoor and outdoor sports? Which do you prefer? Give reasons for your choice.
4. Why do you think that sports such as snowboarding and rock climbing are becoming more popular?

Paired Readings

▶ In this section, you will find two different stories on the same theme. Choose one of the stories to read. Prepare to explain the story to someone who read the same story and then to a person who read the other story.

The readings are about two popular sports in North America today. Work with a partner who is reading the same text. Read and find out about the sport and whom it attracts.

1 In the Winter: The Thrill of Snowboarding

Getting
Information
from
Illustrations

▶ Work with a partner and compare the similarities and differences between the two pictures in the reading on page 132.

1. What are the people doing?
2. How are the people dressed?
3. Which sport would you prefer? Explain your reasons.

Understanding the Main Ideas   ▶ Read all of the paragraphs that follow. Write the number of the paragraph that best fits each of these main ideas.

a. _____ On the ski slopes, people have different reactions to snowboarders.

b. _____ Snowboarders are joining skiers on the mountains.

c. _____ Snowboarding is now becoming a very popular sport for young and old.

Understanding Details   ▶ Answer the questions after each paragraph. In the story, underline the facts that support your answer. Write the question number in the margin of the reading.

A Thrilling Sport Catches On

❶   In the winter, skiing is traditionally a popular sport for people of all ages who like to be outdoors. People take their ski equipment and head for the mountains. But these days, skiers are not the only people on the hills. Snowboarders are joining the skiers for some winter thrills. Snowboarding is fun and exciting. It is like surfing on the snow. Snowboards are wide, like surfboards, and there are places on the boards to strap them to your feet. You stand on the board and ride the snow like the surfers who ride the ocean waves. Snowboarders move back and forth in wide curves. Snowboarders like to jump and turn as they speed down the mountains.

1. Where do skiers and snowboarders go in the winter?

    _____

2. Why do people like snowboarding?

    _____

3. What do snowboards look like?

    _____

4. How do people ride a snowboard?

    _____

5. What do people like to do on snowboards?

    _____

❷   The first people to try snowboarding were young people in their teens and twenties. They liked this innovative sport because it was fast and challenging. They could do special tricks on the board, such as turning in the air or jumping over bumps in the snow. These young snowboarders wore special clothes and used a special vocabulary to talk about their moves. For example, they called themselves "shredders" because they would shred, or tear up, the snow as they moved. When snowboarding first started, skiers did not like the young "shredders." The skiers didn't like the snowboarders' fast and unusual movements. Sometimes, snowboarders damaged the ski paths and made it dangerous for the skiers coming down the mountain. Skiers didn't understand the language and the attitude of snowboarders. Some ski resorts banned snowboarders and didn't allow them on the hills, because of the skiers' complaints.

1. Who were the first people to try snowboarding?

    _____

2. Why did they like snowboarding?

    _____

3. What did snowboarders wear, and how did they talk?

    _____

4. How did skiers feel about snowboarders, and why did they feel this way?

    _____

5. What did ski resorts do, and why did they do this?

    _____

❸   But today, things are different. Snowboarding is becoming more and more popular. Some people think that in the next five years, seventy-five percent of the people who visit ski resorts will be snowboarders. In the United States, the number of snowboarders has grown to over two million people in the last four years. Now snowboarders can compete internationally because it has become an Olympic sport. These young Olympic athletes compete to see who is the best at special events where they expertly twist and turn in the air. And it's no longer a sport that's just for the young. Now when you visit the ski slopes, you'll see people of all ages who are learning to snowboard. For example, there are lessons for mothers and business people. The average age for people who are learning is forty, and the number of people trying the sport is up 200 percent. Some people think that it is easy to learn how to snowboard—even easier than learning to ski. It takes less time and it takes less equipment. Now ski resorts welcome snowboarders to share the hills with skiers.

1. What do people think will happen in the next five years?

   _____

2. Where and how can snowboarders compete?

   _____

3. Who can learn to snowboard?

   _____

4. What are some examples of people who can learn to snowboard?

   _____

5. a. How do ski resorts now feel about snowboarders?

   _____

   b. What is the reason that ski resorts welcome snowboarders?

   _____

   ⏺ Work with a partner. Take turns reading the questions and answers to each other. Refer to the reading if your answers are different.

Recapping the Story

▶ **Note Taking: Listing the Facts** In note form, list the facts from each of the paragraphs. To make your notes, reread the information, and underline the key words in the story.

> *Example:* In the <u>winter</u>, <u>skiing</u> is traditionally a <u>popular sport</u> for <u>people of all ages</u> who like to be <u>outdoors</u>. People take their ski equipment and head for the mountains. But these days, skiers are not the only people on the hills. <u>Snowboarders</u> are <u>joining</u> the <u>skiers</u> for some winter thrills. <u>Snowboarding</u> is <u>fun</u> and <u>exciting</u>. It is like <u>surfing</u> <u>on the snow</u>.

▶ Use the key words you underlined to make an outline, a plan that shows the order of the information, as in the following example:

Paragraph 1
1. skiing
   popular sport for people of all ages
   outdoors, winter
2. snowboarding
   fun and exciting
   surfing on the snow

▶ Work with a partner who read the same information. Take turns explaining the information for each paragraph. Use your outline and notes to help you remember the facts in order, but do not simply read your outline. Tell your partner as much as you can remember. Ask for help if you forget or give incorrect information.

Reacting to the Story

▶ Discuss these questions with a partner.

1. Would you ever try snowboarding? Why or why not?
2. What kind of people do you think should or shouldn't try snowboarding?
3. Do you think that snowboarding will continue to be popular?
4. Is snowboarding dangerous? What safety rules should resorts make for the people who come to ski or snowboard?

❷In the City: Climbing the Wall

Getting Information from Illustrations

▶ Work with a partner and compare the similarities and differences between the two pictures in the reading on page 137. Together, answer these questions:

1. What are these people doing?
2. Where are they?
3. What equipment are they using?
4. How do they feel as they are climbing?
5. How do they feel when they finish?
6. Why do you think people like this sport? Would you like it?
7. Would you like indoor or outdoor climbing?

Understanding the Main Ideas

▶ Read all of the paragraphs. Write the number of the paragraph that best fits each of these main ideas.

a. _____ There are many reasons why climbing is good for you.

b. _____ Climbing the wall is not a very difficult sport if you have the right equipment and attitude.

c. _____ More people are finding out that they can learn to climb in the city.

Understanding Details

▶ Answer the questions after each paragraph. In the story, underline the facts that support your answer. Write the question number in the margin of the reading.

Overcoming Fear

❶   Rock climbing is a popular sport. Many Americans are putting on climbing boots and other climbing equipment to walk up the side of a mountain. How did this sport become so popular? Where do people learn the skill of climbing? Many people learn outdoors in parks or other places. But if you think that you have to go to the mountains to learn how to climb, you're wrong. Many Americans are learning to climb in city gyms. Here, with the help of trained instructors, people are learning on special climbing walls. The climbing wall goes straight up and has small holding places for hands and feet.

1. What do you need to wear to go climbing?

   _____

2. Where do many people go to learn the skill of climbing?

   a. outdoors _____

   b. indoors _____

3. What does a climbing wall look like?

   _____

❷   How do people climb the wall? To climb, you need special shoes and a harness around your chest to hold you. There are ropes to attach to your harness. The ropes hold you in place so that you don't fall. A beginner's wall is usually about fifteen feet high, and you climb straight up. There are small pieces of metal that stick out for you to stand on and hold on to. Sometimes it's easy to see the next piece of metal. Sometimes, it's not. The most difficult part is controlling your fear. Fear of falling is a normal human reaction, so it's difficult not to feel fear. But when you move away from the wall, the harness and the ropes hold you, and you begin to feel safe. The equipment enables you to move. You move slowly and carefully until you reach the top. At the top, the instructor slowly releases the rope, and then you slide back to the floor. Your arms and legs feel tired, but you feel great. Learning to climb is not very difficult.

1. What equipment do you need to climb the wall?

_____

2. What are the ropes for?

_____

3. Where do you put your hands and feet on the wall?

_____

4. What is the most difficult part and why?

_____

5. What happens when you move away from the wall?

_____

6. What happens at the end, and how do you feel?

_____

❸   Climbing attracts people because it is good exercise. You don't have to be a super athlete to climb the wall. It's good exercise for almost anyone. You use your whole body, especially your arms and legs. This sport gives your body a complete workout. When you climb, you strengthen your mind as well as your body. Climbing demands discipline. And it demands concern for safety and security. It teaches you the importance of cooperation. It gives you a chance to slow down and still feel challenged. This is a sport for people who like a challenge.

1. Why do people like to climb?

_____

2. What kind of people can be good climbers?

_____

3. What parts of the body do you use in climbing?

_____

4. Why is this sport good for you?

_____

◉ Work with a partner. Take turns reading the questions and answers. Refer to the information in the reading if you have different answers.

Recapping the Story

◉ **Note Taking: Listing the Facts** In note form, list the facts from each of the paragraphs. To make your notes, reread the information, and underline the key words in the story.

Example: Rock climbing is a popular sport. Many Americans are putting on climbing boots and other climbing equipment to walk up the side of a mountain. How did this sport become so popular? Where do people learn the skill of climbing? Many people learn outdoors in parks or other places.

◉ Use the key words you underlined to make an outline, a plan that shows the order of the information as in the following example:

Paragraph 1
1. Rock climbing
    popular
    climbing boots and equipment
    walk up … side of a mountain
2. How … become popular
3. Where do people learn
    outdoors in parks or other places

◉ Work with a partner who read the same information. Take turns explaining the information for each paragraph. Use your outline notes to help you remember the facts in order, but do not simply read your outline. Tell your partner as much as you can remember. Ask for help if you forget or give incorrect information.

Reacting to the Story

◉ Discuss these questions with a partner.

1. Would you try indoor or outdoor climbing? Why or why not?
2. What kind of people do you think should or shouldn't try climbing?
3. What do you think is easy or difficult about climbing? Why is it popular?
4. Do you think that climbing is dangerous? Why or why not?

❶Comparing the Readings

Completing the Chart   ▶ **A** Work with a partner who read a different story. Together, ask each other questions, and use your notes to complete the chart.

Questions	Snowboarding	Climbing
1. What do you have to do to learn this sport?		
2. What kind of equipment do you need to have?		
3. What kinds of people can learn this sport?		
4. Where and when can you practice this sport?		
5. Is this an Olympic sport?		
6. What is the challenge of this sport?		
7. Why is this sport popular?		

▶ From the information in the chart, circle the things that are similar about these two sports. Prepare to explain this information to the class.

▶ **B** **Role Play** Think of a new sport, such as beach volleyball, ultimate frisbee, or kite surfing, that you think is fun to do. Give four or five reasons you think a person should try this new sport. Explain the sport—how you play, what the rules are, where you play, what equipment you need, and so on—and write your list of reasons.

For example: It's easy to learn this sport. It's a really fun sport if you like a challenge. It's not expensive to play. You can meet new people.

▶ Work with a partner and take turns convincing each other to try this sport. Ask questions about the sport to find out as many details as possible.

▶Vocabulary Building

**Word Form
and Meaning**

▶ **A** Match the words in Column A with their meanings in Column B.

Column A

_____ 1. cooperate

_____ 2. enable

_____ 3. innovate

_____ 4. instruct

_____ 5. secure

Column B

a. to develop something new

b. to teach someone or something

c. to join together for a common purpose

d. to protect from danger

e. to make something possible

▶ **B** Study these five words in their various forms: verb, noun, adjective, and adverb. The forms are not in the same order in each column. Then choose the correct form to fill out the chart below. These words are commonly found in general and academic texts.

cooperate (v.)	enable (v.)	innovate (v.)	instruct (v.)	secure (v.)
cooperation (n.)	enabler	innovatively	instructor	security
cooperative (n.)	enabling	innovation	instructional	securely
cooperative (adj.)	enabled	innovator	instructing	secure
cooperating (adj.)		innovative	instructed	secured
cooperatively (adv.)		innovating	instruction	securer

Verb	Noun	Adjective	Adverb
enable	1.	1.	
		2.	
innovate	1.	1.	1.
	2.	2.	
instruct	1.	1.	
	2.	2.	
		3.	
secure	1.	1.	1.
	2.	2.	

▶ Compare lists with a partner. Try to agree on the same answers.

▶ **C** Write three sentences using words from the list.

Vocabulary in Context

▶ **A** Complete each statement with one of the adjectives from the readings. In the sentence, underline the words that helped you to make your choice. Circle the word in the reading.

1. The skiers didn't like the snowboarders' _____ and unusual movements.

2. The _____ part of this sport is learning to control one's fear.

3. People learn to climb on _____ _____ walls.

4. The _____ age for people who try this sport is rising.

5. Skiing is a very _____ sport for people who like to be outdoors in the winter.

6. This sport gives your body a _____ workout.

7. Snowboards are _____ like surfboards.

▶ **B Jigsaw Sentences** *When* is a word that introduces a condition or a time period in which an action takes place. *When* can begin a sentence, or it can be within a sentence. For example: When you reach the top, the instructor releases the rope and you slide to the floor. Use your understanding of the ideas to complete these sentences.

▶ Match the beginning of each sentence in Column A with the ending that fits it best in Column B.

Column A

_____ 1. When you move away from the wall,

_____ 2. When you climb,

_____ 3. When you visit the ski slopes,

_____ 4. When snowboarding first started,

Column B

a. skiers didn't like the young "shredders."

b. you'll see that people of all ages are learning to snowboard.

c. you strengthen your mind as well as your body.

d. the harness and the ropes hold you, and you begin to feel safe.

▶ Compare your answers with a partner. Take turns reading your answers.

▶ **C** Write the jigsaw sentences with "when" in the middle.

Example: When you need me, just call.
Just call when you need me.

▶ **D Verb and Prepositions** Complete these verb phrases with the correct preposition from the following list.

a. down (2×)   b. on   c. out   d. in   e. up

1. Small pieces of metal stick _____ from the wall to help you climb.

2. You slide _____ the rope until you reach the floor.

3. To return to their camp above, they had to walk back _____ the mountain.

4. The snowboarders wanted to speed _____ the slopes.

5. They practiced turning _____ the air.

6. In snowboarding you learn to stand _____ the board.

▶ In the reading, find three sentences with verb and preposition combinations. Circle the verb/preposition phrase. Compare your answers with a partner. Take turns reading the sentences.

⒠xpanding Your Language

Reading

There are many different new sports that people can try. One of these is mountainboarding. Read about this new sport and find out how it is becoming popular and why. Notice how much easier it is to understand this now that you have already done some reading on this topic.

▶ Before beginning, read the following questions. After reading, answer them based on the information in the text.

1. Where and when can you go mountainboarding?
2. When did this sport begin?
3. What does a mountainboard look like?
4. How does it move?
5. What kind of people can enjoy this sport?
6. What kind of equipment do you need and why is this needed?
7. How can this sport be practiced safely?

The Thrill of Boarding — Winter and Summer

Snowboarding is a popular winter sport. But you can't snowboard without snow, or can you? It seems that even in the summer you can still enjoy the thrill of boarding down a mountain. Mountainboarding is a sport that is becoming more and more popular.

Mountainboarding began in 1993 as a warm-weather activity. The board is four feet long and has big tires at the front and back that are from nine to twelve inches wide. With these big tires you can roll over small things such as rocks and bumps. Mountainboards can go anywhere—streets, parks, trails, or ski runs. The rider can control the speed of the board by turning the board sharply and often. The movement is just like a snowboard. You can slow down or brake to a stop by using the back of the board and sliding it along the ground. However, this sport is not for everyone. You have to be in good physical shape to control the board on a rocky mountain path. Of course, you need to wear a lot of protective gear. Dirt is a lot harder than snow. It's bumpier than snow, and it hurts more when you fall. To be safe, mountainboarders wear a lot of safety equipment. You need a helmet, elbow pads, knee pads, wrist guards, a chest protector, special pants, gloves, and even a mouth guard to protect your teeth. But mountainboarders like the sport because it feels so exciting to speed down a mountain and jump over bumps. It feels like flying.

Snowboarding and mountainboarding are both good exercise. But you have to be careful. It is important to take time to learn how to ride. It is a good idea to take a course to learn how to ride and how to stop safely. And it is important to have equipment that fits you and will protect you. Experts say that if you do these things, you will be safe.

Speaking

▷ **A Preparing a Questionnaire** Find out what the most popular indoor and outdoor sports are among the students in your class. Choose one set of questions to answer—for indoor or outdoor sports (on the next page). Answer the questions yourself. Then interview two other people and write notes of their answers.

Indoor Sports	You	Student A	Student B
1. What sport do you practice?			
2. Where do you go?			
3. How often?			
4. What equipment do you need?			
5. What training do you need?			
6. How expensive is this sport?			
7. How challenging is it?			

Outdoor Sports	You	Student A	Student B
1. What sport do you practice?			
2. Where do you go?			
3. How often?			
4. What equipment do you need?			
5. What training do you need?			
6. How expensive is this sport?			
7. How challenging is it?			

▶ Form a group and compare your information. Make a report of your group's answers to present to the whole class.

▶ **B Two-Minute Taped Talk**   Record a two-minute audiotape or audio CD about one of the sports you learned about in this chapter. To make your recording, follow the steps on pages 65–66.

Writing

▶ **Personal Reaction**   Write about a sport that you like or would like to try. Describe the sport and explain why you think it is interesting. Explain using as much information as you can.

 *Online Study Center*   For additional activities, go to the *Reading Matters* Online Study Center at *college.hmco.com/pic/wholeyone2e*.

12 Training for the Olympics Today: What Does It Take?

Chapter Openers

Getting Information from a Chart

A Use the information from the chart to answer the following questions about the Olympics then and now.

	Olympics Then	Olympics Now
Year	**1896**	**2004**
Number of athletes	300	11,099
Number of countries	15	202
Events	43	300
Sports	9	28
Who is allowed to compete	Only amateurs	Amateurs and professionals with the largest number of women athletes in history
International press coverage	Very little	On live television around the world with four billion viewers
Training times	A few months; part time	All year; full time

1. Compare the number of athletes at the Olympic Games in the past and in recent years.
2. How many more countries now come to the modern Olympics?
3. What kinds of athletes were allowed in the Games in 1896, and how is that different today?
4. What kind of press coverage do Olympic athletes get today, and how is that different from the past?

▶ **B** Discuss your answers with a partner. Then share your ideas about the following questions.

1. Why do athletes go to the Olympics?
2. How much time and money does an athlete have to spend to get to the Olympics?
3. In comparison with athletes in the past, what do today's athletes know about
   a. how much time to train?
   b. what kind of food to eat?
   c. what kind of equipment to use?
   d. how to prepare themselves mentally?

Exploring and Understanding Reading

Predicting

▶ Read the following statements. Write *P* for statements you think are about athletes of the past and *T* for statements about today's athletes. Write *B* if you think that the statement is true for both.

_____ 1. Athletes train part time for the Olympics.

_____ 2. Sports psychologists help athletes improve through mental training.

_____ 3. Athletes train without special equipment or coaches.

_____ 4. Athletes train for a long time.

_____ 5. Athletes show determination and self-sacrifice.

_____ 6. Athletes know the science of how the body produces energy.

_____ 7. Athletes use video cameras to study their performance.

_____ 8. Athletes can improve their performances in small amounts over time.

_____ 9. Athletes represent their countries at the games.

▶ Compare your answers with a partner. Try to agree on the same answers. Review your answers after you finish the reading. Make any changes necessary.

Reaching for Olympic Gold: Past and Present

❶   In the past, people who participated in the Olympics worked on their training part time. Many athletes trained at a university. They practiced their sport while they were studying. Some trained on their own, without special coaches or equipment. They scheduled intense daily training sessions for only a few months before the Games. For the athletes who competed in past Olympics, training was an individual responsibility. Like the athletes of today, to reach the top of any sport, athletes needed determination and self-sacrifice. It takes physical and mental training. The goals and aspirations of today's athletes are no different from those of the past. But today, training for the Olympics is a full-time job. It requires total commitment. Training today is completely different from the way it was in the past.

❷   Today's athletes have much more knowledge about how their bodies perform than the athletes of the past did. Science can now show us how our bodies produce energy. But the amount of energy depends on how long a person trains. Today's athletes have to train for a long time to improve. Coaches can help athletes make important training decisions.

Athletes need to follow a schedule and work continuously at improving. They have to get the right amount of sleep and to eat the right food. Sometimes, they have to get up early in the morning and train for hours before going to school or work. Coaches use video cameras and computers to record an athlete's movements. With their coaches, athletes analyze and study how to move their bodies so that they will improve their performance. The improvement they make is small. But at the Olympics, small improvements can make a big difference. A few seconds is all that separates getting a medal and not getting a medal. The athletes' equipment uses the latest in technology. For example, the bicycle that athletes use is made from carbon fiber and has special tires that are very expensive. Testing the equipment is very expensive. Bicycles were studied in a wind tunnel at a cost of $40,000 an hour.

❸ Today, athletes are learning how to use their minds as well as their bodies. Sports psychologists help athletes improve their performances through mental training by teaching them how to concentrate. They know that our minds and our bodies are linked and work together. Attitude and alertness affect athletic performance. Coaches use this knowledge to show athletes how to raise their self-esteem, their motivation, and their concentration. They can teach them how to visualize, or "see," themselves winning. Athletes can learn these skills and improve their performances. Elizabeth Manley is a good example of an athlete who improved with the help of psychological training. Elizabeth was a talented figure skater. She skated well at practice but she didn't do her best at competitions. It was very frustrating. She decided to use a sports psychologist to help her prepare. The psychologist helped her to imagine herself giving a perfect performance. She trained with the psychologist for a year before the 1988 Winter Olympics competition. Before she went on the ice at the Olympics, she practiced her routine in her mind. The mental work paid off. She had a silver medal at the end of the competition. Dan O'Brian is another good example of an athlete who improved because of a positive mental attitude. Dan was a talented athlete competing in the decathlon, an event that includes pole vaulting. In 1992, he missed qualifying for the pole vaulting event at the Olympic trials. But he was determined. Although he was upset, he put it behind him and focused mentally on what he needed to do for the next four years. He surrounded himself with people who shared his vision of himself. He went on to become the Olympic Decathlon Gold Medal Winner in 2000. Today, many athletes use psychological training to get the competitive edge they need to win.

**Understanding
the Main Ideas**

◐ Write the letter of the paragraph that best fits each of these main ideas.

a. _____ Sports psychologists can help athletes to do their best.

b. _____ Olympic training today is very different from the way it was in the past.

c. _____ Athletes today need to know a lot about how to train for their sport.

**Identifying
Supporting
Points and
Details**

> **Reading Tip**

Some information, such as sub-, or **supporting, points** of a main idea, is more general than other information, such as dates, numbers, or other details. Noticing this type of difference will **help you to relate ideas to one another** as you read. ▪

◐ Read each statement and decide whether it is a supporting (sub-) point or a detail. Refer to the reading to help you decide. Write *S* for supporting points and *D* for details.

_____ 1. Today's athletes have to train for a long time to improve.

_____ 2. Sometimes, they have to get up early in the morning and train for hours before going to school or work.

_____ 3. A few seconds are all that separate getting a medal or not getting a medal.

_____ 4. At the Olympics, small improvements can make a big difference.

_____ 5. Sports psychologists help athletes to improve their performances through mental training.

_____ 6. She skated well in practices, but she didn't do her best at competitions.

_____ 7. Dan O'Brian is another good example of an athlete who improved because of a positive mental attitude.

◐ Compare your answers with a partner. Try to agree on the same answers.

Using Information to Complete a Chart

▶ Find information in paragraphs 1 and 2 to complete this chart. Write the details in note form, as shown in the following examples.

Athletes in the Past	Athletes Today
Worked on their training part time	Train for a long time to improve
Trained at university	Follow a schedule and keep training continuously

▶ Work with a partner. Check to make sure that your information is the same. Take turns telling about the training of athletes today and in the past.

Applying the Information

▶ **Problem Solving** Read the following short interviews with young athletes and decide whether they should

1. get the help of a sports psychologist.
2. get the help of a training coach.

▶ Give reasons based on the interview and information from the first reading.

Interview A

Interviewer: How long have you been training?

Athlete: Twelve years. I started when I was five years old.

Interviewer: Will you compete in the next Olympics?

Athlete: Yes, I am on the team. We're training now.

Interviewer: I watched your training session. It was wonderful; you did everything perfectly.

Athlete: Thanks. But I still have to work hard.

Interviewer: What is the most difficult part for you?

Athlete: The most difficult part isn't the training. It's the competition.

Interviewer: What happens in the competitions?

Athlete: I'm not sure. Sometimes I freeze and my performance isn't good enough. I do better in training.

Interviewer: Do you need to spend more time training?

Athlete: I'm not sure. I spend four hours a day now. Maybe I need something else.

Your suggestion: _____

Reasons why: _____

Interview B

Interviewer: How long have you been training?

Athlete: Twelve years. I started when I was five years old.

Interviewer: Will you compete in the next Olympics?

Athlete: Yes, I am on the team. We're training now.

Interviewer: I watched your training session. It was wonderful; you did everything perfectly.

Athlete: Thanks. But I still have to work hard.

Interviewer: What is the most difficult part for you?

Athlete: The most difficult part is making improvement in my time. I want to finish at least thirty seconds faster.

Interviewer: What happens in the competitions?

Athlete: I need to have more energy at the end. It's the last minute or so that is difficult for me.

Interviewer: Do you need to spend more time training?

Athlete: I'm not sure. I spend four hours a day now. Maybe I'm doing something wrong.

Your suggestion: _____

Reasons why: _____

▶ Compare your suggestions with others. Be prepared to give the reasons for your suggestions.

Discussion Questions

▶ **The Olympic Experience** Think about these questions. Discuss your ideas with a partner or a small group.

1. What are three important reasons that people become Olympic athletes?
2. What rewards do Olympic athletes enjoy?
3. What difficulties do Olympic athletes experience?
4. What problems have the Olympics had? What are the reasons for these problems?
5. What do you think will be the future of the Olympics?

❶Vocabulary Building

**Word Form
and Meaning**

❂ **A** Match the words in Column A with their meanings in Column B.

Column A

Column B

_____ 1. commit

a. to make something technological

_____ 2. qualify

b. to make a plan

_____ 3. require

c. to dedicate yourself to something or someone

_____ 4. schedule

d. to reach an acceptable level

_____ 5. technologize

e. to demand something

❂ **B** Study these five words in their various forms: verb, noun, adjective, and adverb. The forms are not in the same order in each column. Then choose the correct form to fill out the chart below. These words are commonly found in general and academic texts.

commit (v.)	qualify (v.)	require (v.)	schedule (v.)	technologize (v.)
commitment (n.)	qualifiedly	requirement	scheduled	technological
committed (adj.)	qualification	required	scheduler	technology
committing (adj.)	qualifying	requiring	scheduling	technologist
	qualified		schedule	technologically
	qualifier			

Verb	Noun	Adjective	Adverb
qualify	1. 2.	1. 2.	1.
require	1.	1. 2.	
schedule	1. 2.	1. 2.	
technologize	1. 2.	1.	1.

❂ Compare lists with a partner. Try to agree on the same answers.

▶ **C** Write three sentences using words from the list.

▶ **D** **Verbs: Present and Past** Write the past form of the following verbs. Circle these past tense verbs in the reading.

1. compete   _____

2. decide   _____

3. improve   _____

4. link   _____

5. need   _____

6. participate   _____

7. share   _____

8. study   _____

9. surround   _____

10. train   _____

▶ Compare your answers with a partner. Write three sentences and three questions of your own, using both the present and past forms of any of these verbs.

Vocabulary in Context

▶ **A** **Past and Present** Decide whether the sentence needs a verb in the present or in the past or both. Write the correct form of the verb on the line provided. In the sentence, circle the words that helped you make your decision.

1. train

   Today, people _____ very differently from the way

   they _____ at the beginning of the century.

2. produce

   Unlike in the past, we now know a lot about how the body _____ energy.

3. go

   Before she _____ on the ice, she asked her coach to help her to concentrate.

4. take

As in the past, it _____ years of hard work to reach the top of any sport.

5. teach

Now they _____ athletes by using computers and video

equipment. It's very different from the way that they _____ before.

▶ Compare your answers with a partner. Then take turns reading your sentences.

▶ **B** Complete each sentence with one of the words from the following list. In the reading, underline the words that helped you to choose your answer.

a. competition　b. confidence　c. difference　d. improvement
e. knowledge　f. motivation　g. performance　h. self-esteem

1. The coach taught me not to think about the crowds of people

watching but to concentrate on giving the best _____ I could.

2. I did very well at practice, but now I needed to do well in the

_____.

3. He didn't do as well as he could have, because he lost _____ in himself.

4. I had the _____ to do well, but I worried that I hadn't spent enough time training.

5. The coach told her that she could make a small _____ in her game.

6. The _____ between his ability before he trained and after was amazing.

7. Today, we have much more _____ about what is going on in the body than we did before.

8. I needed to think well of myself and to raise my own _____.

▶ Check your answers with a partner. Take turns reading your sentences.

Expanding Your Language

Reading

The ideas of sports psychology are becoming very popular not only with professional athletes but also with ordinary athletes. Read about sports psychology and find out what the experts have to say. Notice how much easier it is to understand this now that you have already done some reading on this topic.

▷ Before beginning, read the following questions. After reading, answer them based on the information in the text.

1. Why is playing team sports as a child important later in life?
2. What responsibility do parents have?
3. What is one of the important skills children learn by being part of a team?
4. What do children have to learn in order for the team to win?
5. How many children were studied in the United States and why was the study done?
6. What were the number one and number ten reasons children gave for playing sports?
7. Why should kids replace the idea of winning with the idea of succeeding?
8. Who should kids try to compete against?
9. How did Lloyd Eisner's parents influence his love of his sport?

The Difference Between Winning and Succeeding

Psychologists know that children learn important life lessons when they participate in sports. Some research even shows that what children learn when they take part in a team sport, such as soccer or basketball, will directly influence how they approach life as adults. More importantly, it is the parents' responsibility to provide kids with the opportunities to develop skills that will help them later in life. What do children learn when they participate in a team sport? One of the skills is how to find a healthy balance between competing and cooperating. All sports are competitions and there is always going to be a winner and a loser. But in order to win, individuals have to put aside what they want for themselves and do what they need to do for the good of the team. Most kids understand that the games they play are competitive. But many kids understand that winning isn't everything. A U.S. study of 26,000 children aged 10–18 who were involved in sports found that winning was only the tenth most important reason for playing on a team. More important reasons were developing skills, being part of the team, and feeling the thrill of playing the game. Having fun was the top reason.

The goal, then, of sports programs and the parents of kids who participate should be to emphasize something other than winning. Sports psychologists suggest replacing the idea of winning with the idea of succeeding. Succeeding means doing your best. Doing your best is not the same as winning. An important part of "doing your best" means trying to improve on your last performance. Bettering your own time, trying to get to your "personal best," is something that everyone can enjoy. Psychologists say that Olympic and professional athletes don't talk about winning. They talk about how they love the sport. Canadian Lloyd Eisner, an Olympic pairs skater, is a good example. He remembers how, when he was a kid, his parents would never force him to go to the ice rink to practice. "Their attitude was, if I didn't want to, I didn't have to. The result was that when I did go, I knew it was my choice. I went because I loved it."

Speaking

▶ **Role Play** Work with a partner. Choose the role of an athlete and a sports psychologist or coach. Together, write out the conversation between these two people, based on the chapter readings and information of your own.

For example, the athlete could be looking for someone to help increase his or her self-esteem and improve performance at competitions. Or an athlete could be looking for someone to help him or her have a better result in training. Here is one example of how to start the conversation:

Athlete:　I need help to do better when I have to compete. Can you help me?
Coach:　I think I can help. I'm a sports psychologist.
Athlete:　How can you help me?

▶ **1.** Practice your role play with your partner. Prepare to present it to others in a small group.

　2. Find another partner and take roles in each other's scenario.

Writing

▶ **Topic Writing** From the information in this chapter or based on your own interests, write about a topic of your choice or one of the following possible topics:

How Athletes of Today Train for their Sport
The Olympics in the Past

To write about your topic, follow these steps:

▶ **1.** Decide on the topic of your essay. Make notes of the information you want to include in your writing. Make an outline using these facts. An outline showing the supporting points for a comparison of present and past Olympic training is shown in the following example.

Olympic Training Today
   1. How many athletes and sports
   2. Training
     a. Types
     b. Where
     c. How long
     d. Expense
   3. Problems

Olympic Training in the Past
   1. How many athletes and sports
   2. Training
     a. Where
     b. How long
     c. Expense
   3. Problems

2. Work with a partner. Use your outline to tell your partner what you plan to write about. Ask your partner whether the information is clear or whether you should add any ideas to make the information more complete.

3. Use your notes to help you organize your writing. Write as much as you can. Write in complete sentences. Refer to the exercise in Chapter 3, page 39, to help you write your sentences.

▶Read On: **Taking It Further**

Reading Cloze   ▷ Use the words from the unit listed here to fill in the blanks in this paragraph.

a. best	b. better	c. earlier (2×)	d. free	e. hard
f. long	g. longer	h. many (2×)	i. older	j. young

What makes an athlete great? According to many coaches, athletes have to work (1) _____ and work (2) _____ hours to reach their goals. The (3) _____ an athlete works at training, the (4) _____ that athlete will be. Most athletes have to face (5) _____ demands. They often get up (6) _____ than most people. They also go to bed (7) _____ and do not go for a night out with friends very often. Many of the (8) _____ athletes start training when they are still young. These (9) _____ athletes can have (10) _____ problems as they get (11) _____. They haven't had enough time to learn how to manage their (12) _____ time or to develop other interests in their life.

▷ Compare your answers with a partner. Try to agree on the same answers.

Reading Journal

> ➤ Reading Tip

Don't forget to write in your **reading journal** and to enter new words for this chapter in your **vocabulary log**. Show your journal and log entries to your teacher. ■

Some very interesting stories have been written about famous athletes of the past, such as Muhammad Ali or Wayne Gretsky. You can find these and other stories in easy-reader texts that your teacher can suggest.

▷ Choose a story about an athlete or a sport that you are interested in. Read the story and then use your reading journal to write some information about what you read. Prepare to tell a partner about the important facts of the story. Show your journal entries to your teacher.

Word Play

 **1.** Choose five to seven new words that you would like to learn from the readings in the unit. Try to choose words that are important, such as the nouns, verbs, and adjectives in a sentence. Make a list of these new words. Write a sentence using each of the words from your list. Underline the new word you used. Write the meaning of the word, its *definition*. Check the work with your teacher.

2. Work with a partner. Tell your partner the definition of the word, the first letter of its spelling, and the number of letters in the word. Ask your partner to guess the word and to give the correct spelling. Continue to give the letters of the word until your partner makes a correct guess.

Online Study Center   For additional activities, go to the *Reading Matters* Online Study Center at *college.hmco.com/pic/wholeyone2e.*

Technology for Today's World

> Nothing is impossible.
>
> —*Lewis Mumford*

Introducing the Topic

Much of what we use every day was invented in the last twenty to thirty years. It doesn't take long for us to become familiar with new technology. Then it doesn't take long for us to need it in our lives. Chapter 13 introduces a new way to grow food. Chapter 14 compares the pros and cons of cell phones and e-mail in our daily lives. Chapter 15 shows one way that the Internet is bringing families closer.

Points of Interest

What kinds of technology do you think have greatly changed our world? Give as many ideas as you can.

13 Food for the Twenty-First Century

Questionnaire ▶ Answer these questions for yourself. Ask two classmates these same questions.

Questions	You	Student A	Student B
1. What are your favorite foods?			
2. What are the various ways we process food to keep it fresh?			
3. What food can we grow today without soil and water (hydroponically)?			
4. What would you eat if you lived in a space colony?			
5. Where would your food come from?			
6. In the future, why will it be important to find new ways to grow and process food?			

▶ Work with a partner. Take turns telling each other about the information you gathered in your questionnaire.

Exploring and Understanding Reading

Agree or Disagree?

▷ Write *A* if you agree or *D* if you disagree with the statements. Give the reasons for your answers.

_____ 1. We can grow food in space colonies.

_____ 2. We can grow lettuce and tomatoes in cold weather.

_____ 3. We need sunlight to grow food.

_____ 4. We can grow food by using chemicals.

_____ 5. We can make delicious meals without using meat.

Previewing

▷ Read the title and the first and last sentences of each paragraph in the reading. From the following list, check (✔) the ideas you expect to find out about in this reading.

_____ 1. Growing food on the earth

_____ 2. Growing food in space colonies

_____ 3. Growing hydroponic vegetables

_____ 4. Making recipes with hydroponic foods

_____ 5. Making meals for fancy restaurants

_____ 6. Experiments with recipes for space-age meals

▷ Compare your choices with a partner. Try to agree on your answers. Read the complete article. Return to the preview list and change or add to the ideas you checked.

What's for Dinner?

❶   Do you want something different for dinner? Try some space food. Scientists are experimenting with ways to grow food in space. Scientists think that in twenty or thirty years, astronauts will be able to live in space colonies off the planet. Already many scientists are living for months on the International Space Station high above the earth. It's too expensive to carry food to feed people living in space colonies. People in space colonies will need to grow food for themselves. But how can they grow food without soil and sunlight?

❷   Today, we already have hydroponic vegetables. These are vegetables you can grow without soil. The food can grow in an artificial environment. The science of hydroponics is not new. Many writers believe that the Hanging Gardens of Babylon were actually a large hydroponic system. This system could have used fresh water that was rich in oxygen and minerals for the plants. Hydroponic systems need light. In addition to sunlight, hydroponic farms can use artificial lights. Instead of soil, hydroponic farms can use special material, such as charcoal and mixtures of chemicals, to feed the plants. And in addition to a natural climate, most hydroponic farms often use greenhouses. One advantage of hydroponics is that diseases and insects that travel through the soil are eliminated. Another advantage—no weeds to pull out.

❸   Farmers know how to grow a few kinds of hydroponic vegetables. In winter, when it is too cold to grow vegetables outdoors, hydroponic farmers can grow such vegetables as lettuce, tomatoes, and cucumbers and many different herbs and spices. These products are in many supermarkets. But in space, people will need to eat more than salad and spices. So scientists are learning how to grow hydroponic rice, beans, potatoes, and wheat. Scientists can even grow hydroponic melons and strawberries. As they conduct these experiments, they are analyzing their results and examining how to apply these results to a real life situation—providing tasty meals for space travelers.

❹   Nutrition scientists at Cornell University in New York State are experimenting with recipes that use these hydroponic vegetables. The National Aeronautics and Space Agency (NASA) is paying for this nutrition research. The scientists are trying to develop new systems that will increase the flavor and the vitamin content of the foods they grow. Some of the Cornell experiments in cooking are unusual. They make imitation meat dishes, such as carrot drumsticks, made from carrots, peppers, onions, garlic, herbs, and bread crumbs, instead of chicken. They make dishes made from tofu and seitan (a wheat protein) instead of meat. How do these unusual foods taste? The scientists invite a group of taste testers into their laboratories. Every week, twenty-five people come to taste five different dishes. So far, they have tested 200 different recipes. The carrot drumstick dish was a hit. It rated an eight out of nine. Perhaps soon, people will eat meals made from hydroponic vegetables that are truly out of this world.

Understanding Details

▶ **A** Circle the letter of the correct answer. In the reading, underline the words that support your answer.

1. Scientists are experimenting with
   a. ways to grow food in space colonies.
   b. ways to grow food in the cold weather.
   c. ways to grow food in expensive restaurants.
2. It takes too much _____ to bring food to space colonies.
   a. time   b. money   c. work
3. To grow hydroponic vegetables, you need
   a. chemicals to feed the plants.
   b. sunlight and warm weather.
   c. soil to grow the plants in.

4. You can find hydroponic vegetables in
   a. space laboratories.
   b. outdoor gardens.
   c. many supermarkets.

5. Scientists are experimenting with recipes that use
   a. vegetables instead of meat.
   b. chicken instead of tofu.
   c. chicken drumsticks.

6. Scientists invite _____ to try out their unusual recipes.
   a. taste testers   b. NASA   c. farmers

▶ **B** Answer the following questions. Write the question number in the margin where you found the information for your answer in the reading.

1. Why do scientists want to grow food in space?

   _____

2. To grow hydroponic vegetables, what do people use instead of soil, sunlight, and a natural climate?

   a. _____

   b. _____

   c. _____

3. What do hydroponic farmers grow when it is cold outside?

   _____

4. What kinds of hydroponic vegetables are produced now? What will people need in space?

Hydroponic Vegetables Now	Hydroponic Vegetables for Space Colonies
a. _____	_____
b. _____	_____
c. _____	_____
d. _____	_____

5. What are scientists at Cornell University doing? Explain and give some examples.

   _____

6. a. Who comes to the laboratory every week?

   _____

   b. What do they do?

   _____

   c. What do they decide?

   _____

▶ Work with a partner. Take turns reading the questions and answers. Refer to the reading if you have different answers.

Applying the Information

▶ **Making an Argument** Apply the information from the reading and from your own experience to give your opinion about the topic of this conversation.

   Art: I tasted the most delicious food at Cornell today.
 Judy: What was it?
   Art: Carrot drumsticks.
 Judy: Sounds strange. What's in it?
   Art: It's a vegetarian dish made from carrots, peppers, onions, garlic, herbs, and bread crumbs, instead of chicken.
 Judy: Why are they making this food?

Art: To try out recipes that people can cook from food that they can grow out in space.

Judy: Is that very practical? Are you planning to join a space colony?

Art: You never know.

Judy: It sounds like a waste of money.

Art: I don't agree. Just fifty years ago, no one would have imagined all of the things we can do today. And some of the foods we use every day, such as freeze-dried drinks, were developed as part of the space program.

Judy: But there are so many other important things that we need to do here on Earth.

Art: Sure, but hydroponic food is good for us to grow on Earth, too. I think that the technology that comes from the space program benefits our daily life. Don't you?

1. What are Art and Judy arguing about?

   _____

2. What arguments can you think of *in favor* of the technological developments, such as hydroponic food, for the space program?

   _____

3. What arguments can you think of *against* these space research programs?

   _____

▶ Share your ideas with a partner or with others in a small group. Be prepared to present your ideas to the class.

❭Vocabulary Building

Word Form and Meaning

▶ **A** Match the words in Column A with their meanings in Column B.

Column A

_____ 1. analyze

_____ 2. eliminate

_____ 3. experiment

_____ 4. increase

_____ 5. provide

Column B

a. to remove

b. to give something to someone

c. to add to something

d. to look at something carefully

e. to try something new

▶ **B** Study these five words in their various forms: verb, noun, adjective, and adverb. The forms are not in the same order in each column. Then choose the correct form to fill out the chart below. These words are commonly found in general and academic texts.

analyze (v.)	eliminate (v.)	experiment (v.)	increase (v.)	provide (v.)
analyst (n.)	eliminating	experimenter	increase	provider
analysis (n.)	elimination	experimentation	increasingly	provisional
analyzer (n.)	eliminated	experimental	increased	provision
analyzing (adj.)		experiment	increasing	provisionally
analytic (adj.)				providing
analytically (adv.)				provided

Verb	Noun	Adjective	Adverb
eliminate	1.	1.	
		2.	
experiment	1.	1.	
	2.		
	3.		
increase	1.	1.	1.
		2.	
provide	1.	1.	1.
	2.	2.	
		3.	

▶ Compare lists with a partner. Try to agree on the same answers.

▶ **C** Write three sentences using words from the list.

▶ **D** Many words have more than one form. Look at the different forms for the word *experiment*.

a. **experiment (noun):** a new way to do something
b. **experiment (noun):** a controlled procedure to discover something new
c. **experiment (verb):** to try or to carry out a new procedure

▶ Read the sentences below and write the letter of the correct form on the line provided.

1. _____ He brought all of the results of this latest **experiment** to show his professor.

2. _____ She conducted an **experiment** to test the new technique for growing food.

3. _____ Could you **experiment** with this technique to see if it works?

4. _____ Joan's **experiment** with this new diet was starting to worry her mother.

5. _____ They decided to **experiment** with the seeds their friend had brought.

Vocabulary in Context

▶ **A** Complete each sentence with one of the words from the following list. In the sentence, underline the words that helped you make your choice.

a. artificial   b. hydroponic   c. imitation   d. nutritional   e. unusual

1. You can find fresh _____ vegetables in the supermarket even in the winter.

2. She offered me a new and _____ dish that I had never tasted before.

3. The _____ meat tasted so real that I couldn't believe it was actually tofu.

4. NASA is paying for the _____ research that is developing food for people living in space colonies.

5. They used chemicals and created an _____ environment to grow the food they needed for the winter.

▶ **B** You can find the words *instead of* used in this reading to show that one thing can replace something else.

Complete the following sentences, using words from the reading. Use the meaning of the other words in the sentence to help you make a good guess.

1. Hydroponic farms use _____ instead of sunlight.

2. Instead of _____, hydroponic farms use special mixtures of chemicals.

3. Hydroponic farms can use greenhouses instead of a _____.

4. They can use _____ and _____ instead of meat.

▶ **C** In English, *but* links ideas that are different within the same sentence. An example of this is, "I don't have any meat, *but* I do have fish for supper."

Complete two of the sentences from the preceding list, using *but* to express the contrast.

1. Hydroponic farms don't use sunlight, but they use _____.

2. They don't use meat, but _____.

▶ Compare your answers with a partner. Try to agree on the same answers. Take turns reading your answers.

Expanding Your Language

Reading

▶ **Asking Information Questions** Choose story A, which follows, or story B, which is in the "Exercise Pages" section of the book. Student A works with story A. Student B works with story B on page 248. Complete the following steps.

▶ 1. Read the information questions about your story.

2. Read the story to find the main idea.

3. Underline the important facts that give the answers to the questions.

4. Work with a partner who read the same story to compare the facts you underlined.

5. Take turns asking and answering each other's questions.

6. Write your answers in note form.

7. Use your notes and take turns explaining as much of the story as you can.

Information Questions

1. Who developed this technology?
2. What is it used for?
3. How does it work?
4. What are the benefits?
5. Where is it used?

A: Wheeling Water

   South African architect Hans Hendrikse and his brother Piet, a civil engineer, have invented a new type of wheel. They made a round, thick drum with a hole in the middle. You can fill the drum with water, screw on the lid, and roll the drum along the ground. You can pull the drum with a rope that goes through the middle. With the drum, it is easier to carry water than by the old method of carrying it in buckets or in jars on backs. The brothers called their invention the Q-Drum. You can get the drum in 50- and 70-liter sizes. The invention is now used in Kenya, Ethiopia, Tanzania, Namibia, and South Africa.

Speaking

▶ **1.** Work with a partner who read story B on page 249. Explain your story to each other. Use the illustrations to help you explain. Ask and answer each other's questions.

2. Together, make a list of the similarities and differences between your two stories.

3. Share your ideas with your classmates.

4. Use the questions and answers to help you write about each of the stories.

Online Study Center   For additional activities, go to the ***Reading Matters*** Online Study Center at *college.hmco.com/pic/wholeyone2e*.

New Ways to Keep in Touch

Chapter Openers

Discussion Questions

▶ **Advantages and Disadvantages** Think about these questions. Discuss your ideas with a partner or in a small group.

1. When do you talk on the phone? For what purposes?
2. Would you use a cell phone? Why or why not?
3. What are the advantages and disadvantages of cell phones?
4. When and how often do you send and receive mail?
5. Would you use the Internet to send or receive mail?
6. What are the advantages and disadvantages of e-mail?

Paired Readings

▶ In this section, you will find two different stories on the same theme. Choose one of the two to work with. Prepare to explain the story to someone who read the same story and then to a person who read the other story.

▶ "Keep in touch." Today, it's so easy to do. In fact, with the advances in today's communications systems, we can keep in touch almost all the time. These are readings about the newest means of communicating. Read and find out the advantages and disadvantages of cell phones or e-mail.

①Cell Phones: The Pros and Cons

Getting Information from a Graph

▶ Look at the graph below and answer these questions.

1. How fast are cell phones becoming more popular?

_____

2. Why are sales of cell phones increasing?

_____

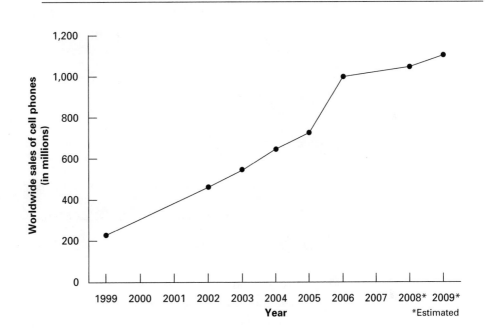

Understanding the Main Ideas

▶ Read all six of the paragraphs. Then write a sentence that expresses the main idea of each paragraph.

1. _____

2. _____

3. _____

4. _____

5. _____

6. _____

Understanding Details

◐ Answer the questions after each group of paragraphs. In the story, underline the facts that support your answers. Write the question number in the margin.

Cell Phones: A Communications Revolution

❶   Do you have to be at home to get a phone call? Not anymore. With a cell (short for cellular) phone, you can call people and receive calls anytime and anywhere. Cell phones use both radio waves and telephone lines. You can get two kinds of phones: analog or digital. Some phones combine both types in one. Cell phones are getting smaller and cheaper. People like the convenience of being able to call anytime from any location. These days almost everyone carries a cell phone.

❷   With today's technology, the features are endless. You can have call waiting (to receive a call while you are already talking) and caller ID, which shows you, on your cell phone, the name of the caller. The cell phone can be your home office. You can send and receive faxes (short for facsimiles, such as documents and other printed material) and make notes to yourself on the phone. You can send small text messages to friends or coworkers—whether they are far away or sitting in the same room. You can take pictures with your phone if you have a camera phone. Taking pictures is probably the most revolutionary way that these "phones" can be used. That means that everyone can take pictures of everyday life. Teenage girls go the salons and take pictures of their haircuts. They send the pictures to their friends to get an instant "good or not" reaction to their new styles. For parents who are busy at work, the cell phone can be connected to a website and act as a video camera. With the camera phone, they can monitor what their teenager is doing. One parent of a six-year-old saw his child ride his bicycle for the first time. He used his phone to take a picture of it and then e-mailed the picture to his wife at work. You could use your phone to check in on an elderly relative or your pet at home.

❸   You can use your cell phone to reach people anywhere in the world. Cell phones are also good in an emergency if you need to call for help. In one case, a couple of mountain climbers got lost after they took the wrong path on a late afternoon hike. They panicked as they realized that night would be closing in soon. Luckily one of the hikers had a cell phone and dialed for emergency help. The police were able to dispatch a rescue crew to help locate and bring the hikers back down to safety.

1. How easy is it to call people and receive calls with a cell phone?

   _____

2. What kinds of cell phones are there, and what do they use to work?

   _____

3. a. What is call waiting? _____

   b. What is caller ID? _____

4. What home office jobs can you do with a cell phone?

   a. _____

   b. _____

5. What is one revolutionary use of cell phones?

   _____

6. What are three examples of this use in everyday life?

   a. _____

   b. _____

   c. _____

7. What is one example of the usefulness of cell phones in an emergency?

   _____

❹   But is it all good news? Not always. What happens when people bring their camera phones to the gym? Some health clubs have decided to ban their members from bringing camera phones into their buildings. People who come there to work out don't want to be photographed. Pictures taken with a camera phone can be put up on the Web. They can be sent to millions of people through the Internet. Businesses are worried also. Some companies have banned camera phones from their factories. These companies are afraid that people will try to steal the design of their products. Another problem is that cell phones depend on other technology to function well. When a communications satellite failed in 1998, some users lost their phone service. Cell phones are dangerous to use when you drive. More and more car accidents happen while people are talking on their cell phones. Cell phone conversations are not private. People can listen in to other people's conversations when they are talking on cell phones. They do this by using a scanner that can pick up the same radio frequency used for the calls. People don't like to hear cell phones ringing when they are at the movies or in a class at school. And people don't like to have to listen to other people's private phone conversations while they are traveling on the bus or standing in line at the supermarket.

❺   Some people think that these phones are transforming our world of correct manners. According to a survey, seventy-one percent of cell phone users are always late for their appointments. Why is this the case? It's just too easy to let people know on a moment-to-moment basis that they will be late. They can send text messages over their phones. They can explain where they are, how fast they will be able to get to their appointment, and exactly when they will be arriving. Text messaging gives us a minute-by-minute diary of our day. Some studies found that the most common text message was "Where are you?"

❻   Last, but not least, some cell phone companies charge quite a bit of money for using the service during certain times. Cell phones can be useful, but they can be expensive, they don't always function when you need them to, and they can be annoying.

1. Where are camera phones banned in health clubs and why?

_____

2. Why are businesses worried about camera phones?

_____

3. What happened to some cell phone users in 1998?

_____

4. Why are cell phones dangerous to use when you drive?

_____

5. When do people not like to hear cell phones ringing?

_____

6. When do people not want to listen to phones ringing or private phone conversations?

_____

7. How are cell phones changing people's need to be on time?

_____

▶ Work with a partner. Take turns reading the questions and answers to each other. Refer to the reading if your answers are different.

Recapping the Story

> **▷ Reading Tip**

Highlighting is a useful strategy for finding and remembering facts and important ideas you read. To highlight, use a colored highlighting pen to mark information. Be careful to mark only the information you want to tell your partner. Use the underlining you did to answer the questions to help you find the information to highlight. ■

▶ **Highlighting** Work with a partner who read the same information. Together, highlight the important facts in both groups of paragraphs. Then use the information to complete this note-taking chart about cell phones.

Questions	Facts
1. How do they work?	
2. Where can they work?	
3. What can you do with them?	
4. What are the advantages?	
5. What are the disadvantages?	

▶ Practice telling the information to your partner. Try not to read the notes as you speak. Ask for help if you forget or give incorrect information.

Reacting to the Story

▶ **A** Make a list of three or four advantages and disadvantages of cell phones. Use the information from the reading and some of your own ideas. Write your ideas in note form, as shown in the example.

Advantages   **Disadvantages**

1. People can call anytime   Depends on other technology

2. _____   _____

3. _____   _____

4. _____   _____

▶ Work with a partner and share your ideas. Together, make a list of your best ideas to share with others.

▶ **B** Discuss these questions with others, and give the reasons for your answers.

1. Are there more advantages or disadvantages to using cell phones?

2. When would you use a cell phone? When wouldn't you use one?

3. How popular will cell phones become in the future?

② E-Mail: The Pros and Cons

Getting Information from a Graph

▶ Look at the graphs below and answer these questions.

1. In the United States, who uses e-mail?

_____

2. Why do you think e-mail use is increasing?

_____

3. How and when do you use e-mail?

_____

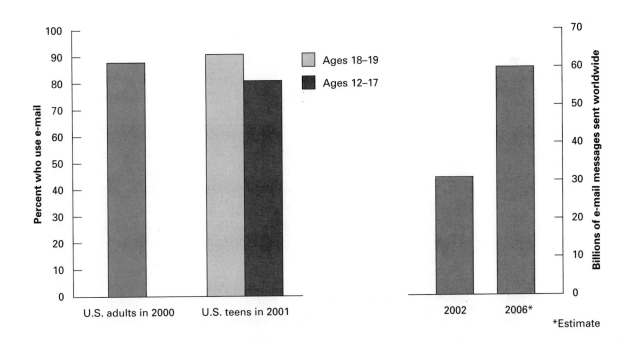

Understanding the Main Ideas

▶ Read all four paragraphs. Write a sentence that expresses the main idea of each paragraph.

1. _____

2. _____

3. _____

4. _____

Understanding Details

▶ Answer the questions after each group of paragraphs. In the story, underline the facts that support your answers. Write the question number in the margin.

Is E-Mail for Everyone?

❶   Do you want to send and receive e-mail (*e* for electronic)? It's easy to do. You can connect your computer and modem to a phone line or cable. Then with a service provider, such as America Online, you can have an e-mail account and write, send, and receive messages. It's the most popular activity on the Internet. It is the most inexpensive way to communicate. You can send messages to people all over the world without paying for a long-distance call. You can select and send birthday cards or other greetings online. With e-mail, you can send a message instantly to anyone else who has an e-mail account—even the President of the United States.

❷   Many companies use e-mail for people in their offices or in other offices to communicate with one another. You can send the same message to fifty people or more. You can set up a network of contacts to send out mass messages to. You can even work without having to go into the office; just connect to your office computer and transfer the files you need to your home computer. E-mail addresses are becoming as common as phone numbers. Many schools and universities give e-mail addresses to their students. You'll find lines to write your e-mail address on many official forms. You can also use the Web to do research online for school projects. If you have a project that you are working on, there is probably a website that you can visit to find information on the topic. To locate the information you are looking for, you need to use a search engine such as Google or AskJeeves. After you enter the key words of your topic into the search engine, it will come up with all the information you need—and probably more. Then you can send the information to your e-mail account for future use.

---

1. What can you do if you have an e-mail account?

   _____

2. Why is e-mail an inexpensive way to communicate with people in other cities, states, and countries?

   _____

3. Whom can you send e-mail to?

_____

4. How many people can you send the same message to?

_____

5. What are two ways that e-mail makes work easier?

a. _____

b. _____

6. How common are e-mail accounts becoming?

_____

7. How is e-mail useful to students using the Internet?

_____

❸   But not everyone is happy about e-mail. Some e-mail is annoying junk mail. People don't want to read messages they aren't interested in. It can take time to check and clear your e-mail box. And in today's fast-paced world, we don't like to waste time. Sometimes, the lines are busy, and it's difficult to get a line and log on. Sometimes, the system crashes and can't be used. Worse than that, some people send messages called "viruses," messages that can enter your computer's hard drive and cause damage. This damage can be very serious. It can harm businesses and can disrupt important communications.

❹   Some people feel that getting e-mail is not as satisfying as getting handwritten mail. These people like to receive handwritten letters and cards in the mail. There can be problems when people make the mistake of sending e-mail to the wrong person. In one case, an office worker complained about his boss in an e-mail to another employee. Then he pressed the wrong key to send it to his colleague, and everyone in the office got the message, including his boss. The office worker didn't lose his job, but it didn't help his problems at work. Some parents worry that their children can use their e-mail to find information on the Internet that is not appropriate for them to see. E-mail can be useful and it can contribute to our lives, but it also makes our lives more complicated.

1. What kind of e-mail messages do people not like to get?

_____

2. How is e-mail wasteful of people's time?

_____

3. What are viruses and why are they dangerous?

_____

4. Why do some people think that e-mail is not satisfying?

_____

5. a. What kind of mistake can people make when they send e-mail?

_____

   b. What is one example of this kind of mistake?

_____

6. What do parents worry about?

_____

▶ Work with a partner. Take turns reading the questions and answers. Refer to the reading if you have different answers.

Recapping the Story

> **Reading Tip**

Highlighting is a useful strategy for finding and remembering facts and important ideas you read. To highlight, use a colored highlighting pen to mark information. Be careful to mark only the information you want to tell your partner. Use the underlining you did to answer the questions to help you find the information to highlight. ■

▶ **Highlighting** Work with a partner who read the same information. Together, highlight the important facts in both groups of paragraphs. Then use the information to complete this note-taking chart about e-mail.

Questions	Facts
1. How does it work?	
2. Where can it work?	
3. What can you do with it?	
4. What are the advantages?	
5. What are the disadvantages?	

▶ Practice telling the information to your partner. Try not to read the notes as you speak. Ask for help if you forget or give incorrect information.

Reacting to the Story

▶ **A** Make a list of three or four advantages and disadvantages of e-mail. Use the information from the reading and some of your own ideas. Write your ideas in note form, as shown in the example.

Advantages

1. People can send messages across long distances.

2. _____

3. _____

4. _____

Disadvantages

You might get junk mail.

_____

_____

_____

▶ Work with a partner and share your ideas. Together, make a list of your best ideas to share with others.

▶ **B** Discuss these questions with others, and give the reasons for your answers.

1. Are there more advantages or disadvantages to using e-mail?
2. When would you want to use e-mail? When wouldn't you want to use it?
3. What do you think will be the future of e-mail?

▶Comparing the Readings

Discussing the Information

▶ **A** Work with a partner who read a different story. Use your notes and your charts to answer the following questions:

1. How does this communications technology work?
2. What are three advantages of this technology?
3. What are three disadvantages of this technology?

▶ **B** **Reacting to the Information** Discuss the questions in the "Reacting to the Story" section for each reading. Explain whether, how, and when you would use these two communication tools.

❶Vocabulary Building

**Word Form
and Meaning**

▶ **A** Match the words in Column A with their meanings in Column B.

Column A

_____ 1. function

_____ 2. monitor

_____ 3. select

_____ 4. transfer

_____ 5. transform

Column B

a. to change something or someone

b. to choose something or someone

c. to move something or someone

d. to watch carefully

e. to act in the proper way

▶ **B** Study these five words in their various forms: verb, noun, adjective, and adverb. The forms are not in the same order in each column. Then choose the correct form to fill out the chart below. These words are commonly found in general and academic texts.

function (v.)	monitor (v.)	select (v.)	transfer (v.)	transform (v.)
function (n.)	monitored	selection	transfer	transformer
functioning (adj.)	monitoring	selectively	transferral	transformational
functional (adj.)	monitor	selected	transfer	transformed
functionally (adv.)		selective	transferred	transforming
		selector	transferring	transformation

Verb	Noun	Adjective	Adverb
monitor	1.	1.	
		2.	
select	1.	1.	1.
	2.	2.	
transfer	1.	1.	
	2.	2.	
		3.	
transform	1.	1.	
	2.	2.	
		3.	

◉ Compare lists with a partner. Try to agree on the same answers.

◉ **C** Write three sentences using words from the list.

Vocabulary in Context

◉ **A** In English, technical terms are often explained by giving an explanation in words that follow. These explanations are set apart by special punctuation, such as commas (,) or parentheses ( ).

◉ Look at the article, underline the technical words, and write the explanations for these terms.

1. e-mail _____

2. cell phones _____

3. faxes _____

4. caller ID _____

5. call waiting _____

6. virus _____

◉ Compare your answers with a partner. Then explain the terms to each other.

◉ **B** Complete each statement with one of the verbs from the following list. Underline the words that helped you to make your choice.

a. complain	b. fail	c. have	d. listen	e. lose
f. operate	g. reach	h. receive	i. send	j. locate

1. People don't like to have to _____ to other people's conversations.

2. This phone costs a lot of money, so be careful and don't _____ it.

3. If the satellite systems _____, we won't be able to make a call.

4. She left me the instructions, but her system looks difficult to

_____.

5. If you need to _____ me, here's the phone number where I'll be.

6. Do you _____ to be at home to get the call, or could you be at work?

7. I don't know how much time it will take to _____ the articles
I need.

8. I finished writing, and now I'm ready to _____ you this letter.

9. I hate to _____, but this machine is not working again today.

10. If you _____ this letter, please send a reply right away.

Expanding Your Language

Reading

There are many different types of new technology that people can try out. One of the areas where technology is changing rapidly is in our cars. Read about this new development and find out what changes are becoming popular and why. Notice how much easier it is to understand this now that you have already done some reading on this topic.

▶ Before beginning, read the following questions. After reading, answer them based on the information in the text.

1. What is Susan King looking for and why?

_____

2. a. What is Susan's job? _____

   b. What must she do to get to work?

   _____

   c. What happens while she is on her way to work?

   _____

3. What does she want to be able to do in her car?

_____

4. What have cars become in recent years?

_____

5. What are some entertainment features that these cars offer?

   a. _____

   b. _____

6. What in-demand features do cars have for business people?

_____

7. What can car manufacturers do to make cars more comfortable?

    _____

8. What can airbag technology do?

    _____

9. What are some things that the on-board computer can help drivers to do?

    a. _____

    b. _____

    c. _____

10. How can night-vision technology help the driver?

    _____

11. a. What is one European company offering?

    _____

    b. What can it do?

    _____

    c. Will this be popular in the United States or not?

    _____

12. What are consumers looking for?

    _____

New Car Comforts

Susan King is looking to buy a new car. She's willing to pay a good price, but only if the car can do double duty as her office. Susan is an accountant who puts in two hours per day traveling to and from her office. She is looking for a car that will allow her to work while she's on the road. After all, while she's in the car, her faxes, e-mail, and phone messages are piling up at the office. She wants a car that will allow her to keep her hands on the wheel while she dictates notes into a machine that can transfer them onto her computer and send them out over e-mail.

There are cars that can do that and more. Most recently, cars have become traveling entertainment and dining centers. There are some cars that have devices that can keep your drinks hot or cold. Some cars also have a mobile screen for videos and for game playing. One car even has a children's activity center. It pulls out of the middle of a seat and has a Lego play surface, a desktop for writing and drawing, and a storage compartment for keeping toys. But the features that are most in demand are those that help busy commuters stay in touch with their work. One feature is an on-board computer that responds to a person's voice. The voice-activated computer makes it possible for a people to dictate letters and memos, send and receive e-mail, and even print out faxes while they are in the car.

Comfort is as much an issue for many drivers as safety is. So car manufacturers are looking at designing seats that move in response to a person's body weight and shape. They are also designing systems that deliver instant heat and cooling. One device stores heat so that warm air can reach front seat passengers ten to fifteen seconds after the car is restarted. Airbag technology makes it possible to determine if someone is in the passenger seat and how close the person is to the airbag. The on-board computer can serve a number of purposes. It can locate your destination and tell you how to get there. It can transmit your location in an emergency and help people get to your aid if you have car trouble. One of the latest safety features is night vision. This system helps drivers see in the dark. It makes objects in the distance more visible to the driver.

Car manufacturers are looking for ways to attract customers to buy their newest vehicles. One European company is trying to interest American manufacturers in a seat that turns into a bed. It makes it easier for passengers to sleep. In Europe, people are used to the idea of pulling over to the side of the road and sleeping. But Americans don't do that—yet. One thing that Americans are looking for is to have technology that is affordable. Consumers want innovation but they are not often willing to pay a lot extra for it. And as much as Susan King is looking for a way to work while she drives, others are not so sure. Some people like the idea of driving without being bothered by the technology that keeps us at work even when we're not in the office.

Speaking

▶ **A Questionnaire** Use these questions to interview two people. You may want to interview people outside your class. Note their answers.

To carry out this activity, follow these steps:

▶ **1.** Practice asking and answering questions.

2. Practice introducing yourself.

3. State the topic of your questionnaire. For example, "My questionnaire is about cell phone and e-mail use."

4. Ask for their permission to ask your questions.

5. Ask your questions. Note all answers in the chart below.

Questions	Student A	Student B
1. Do you use a cell phone?		
2. Do you use e-mail?		
3. What are cell phones useful for? Give one example.		
4. What is e-mail useful for? Give one example.		
5. Can people have problems with cell phones? Give one example.		
6. Can people have problems with e-mail? Give one example.		

▶ Work with a partner or a small group to report on the results of your questionnaire. Share your results with your classmates.

▶ **B Two-Minute Taped Talk** Record a two-minute audiotape or audio CD about one of the communications technologies you learned about in this chapter. To make your recording, follow the steps on pages 65–66.

Writing

▷ Topic Writing: Comparing Technologies Write about one of the technologies explained in this chapter. Write ten to fifteen sentences about how to use this tool and other sentences about the advantages and disadvantages you think are important. Use the notes you prepared and the ideas you discussed in this chapter.

To carry out this task, follow these steps:

▷ 1. Reread your notes and recall all of the information you have gathered from discussions about the advantages and disadvantages of your topic.

2. Make an outline of the information you plan to include. Refer to Chapter 3, page 39, for an example of how to outline.

3. Check your outline against the information in the article.

4. Work with a partner who is writing on the same topic. Use your outline to explain what you plan to write. Make any changes necessary to complete your outline.

5. Write your essay and give it to your teacher.

 *Online Study Center*   For additional activities, go to the *Reading Matters* Online Study Center at *college.hmco.com/pic/wholeyone2e.*

15 The Internet Offers an Eye on Your World

Chapter Openers

Discussion Questions

▶ Think about these questions. Discuss your ideas with a partner or in a small group.

1. What is the Internet? How do people use the Internet today?
2. Can people talk to or see one another over the Internet?
3. What are three positive and negative points about the Internet?

Positive   **Negative**

a. _____   _____

b. _____   _____

c. _____   _____

4. Does the Internet help families to keep in touch with one another or keep them separated from one another? Give as many reasons as possible.

Exploring and Understanding Reading

Predicting

▶ This reading is an interview with a busy young working mother whose son is in a day-care center that has Internet access so that parents can see what the children are doing during the day. From the following list, check (✔) the questions that you think the interviewer will ask. Write one question of your own.

_____ 1. Why did you choose this day-care center for your son?

_____ 2. What work do you do?

_____ 3. Are you successful in your business?

_____ 4. What does your son learn at the day-care center?

_____ 5. Is it expensive to use the Internet?

_____ 6. How often do you use the Internet to look at your son?

_____ 7. Is the Internet system safe?

8. _____

▶ Compare your answers with a partner. Then read the interview and find out whether you predicted any of the questions.

You're Only a Click Away

Today, Sally Oh is interviewing a successful executive, Amy Baines, a working mom who uses the Internet at work to watch her three-year-old son while he is at his day care.

Sally: Tell us about your work and about Harry's schedule while you are at work.

Amy: I work at an advertising agency in New York City. I start work at 9 and finish at 6. I work all week, and sometimes I have to travel. Harry is at the day-care center from 8:30 until 6:30. It's a long day for both of us.

Sally: And you can keep in touch with Harry during the day?

Amy: That's right. I can see him whenever I want.

Sally: How do you get to see Harry during the day? The day-care center isn't near your work.

Amy: The day-care center has a video camera that is connected to a special, secure website. When I want to see him, I can call up the website on my computer and see the center on my screen.

Sally: How does that make you feel?

Amy: Wonderful. For example, when I dropped Harry off at the center yesterday, he started to cry. I had to leave, but he just wouldn't stop crying. I felt bad, but I needed to get to work. Then at work, I was so depressed and worried, I couldn't concentrate. I kept thinking about Harry. So I logged on and went to the website. I could see Harry playing a game, as happy as could be. It made me feel better. What a relief. I could go and concentrate on my work. I had a very productive morning.

Sally: Can anyone visit the website?

Amy: No. You need a special name and password to get into the system.

Sally: Do the day-care workers like it?

Amy: At first, they felt self-conscious. But now, they don't seem to notice. The activity in the day-care center goes on as usual.

Sally: How often do you log on to see your son?

Amy: It depends. Usually about four or five times a day. I just like to see him. I like to know what kind of day he's having.

Sally: Does the camera follow the children everywhere?

Amy: Almost everywhere. It's not on in the room where the children take their naps. Or in the book corner. But if I log on when he's in the book corner or if I don't see him, I ask his teacher and she brings him to a place where I can see him on camera. One time I did that so I could show him off to my boss.

Sally: Is this a good system for the day-care center to have?

Amy: I think so. It's good because I can check in and find out whether the center is doing good work with Harry. I can see for myself whether he is happy and learning and getting enough attention from the teachers. I can confirm whether or not the center is following the educational program that they say they offer. I like what I see (there is a variety of interesting activities, and all of the children get individual attention), so I recommended the center to two friends who were looking for good day care for their kids.

Sally: Are there any other benefits to this system?

Amy: Yes. My parents, who live 2,000 miles away, can log on and see their first grandchild learning to do all of those milestone activities: reading and writing for the first time. One time, for example, my father logged on and Harry wrote, "Hi, Grandpa," and held it up to the screen. My father was so happy. He wrote me an e-mail right away. With the Internet, it's as though we're living in the same house.

Understanding Details

⊙ Answer the following questions. In the interview, underline the parts that support your answer. Mark the question number in the margin.

1. What is Amy's work schedule?

   _____

2. What is Harry's day-care schedule?

   _____

3. When can Amy see Harry at day care? How does she do this?

   _____

4. How does this make Amy feel? Give an example.

   _____

5. Do the day-care workers like the system?

   _____

6. How often does Amy look at her son during the day?

   _____

7. What does Amy think of the quality of education at the center? Give three facts to support your answer.

   _____

   _____

   _____

⊙ Work with a partner. Read your questions and answers. Refer to the reading if you have different answers.

Understanding Examples

▶ In the interview, Amy gives two examples to explain why the Internet service is good for her and Harry. In the reading, locate the information given for these explanations. Write the important details in note form.

Why Amy Likes Harry's Online Day Care

Example 1
Checking on Harry at day care after she dropped him off

What happened:

1st:

2nd:

3rd:

Feelings:

Example 2
Grandparents log on

What happened:

1st:

2nd:

3rd:

Feelings:

▶ Work with a partner. Take turns using your notes to explain what happened in these examples.

Applying the Information

▶ **Problem Solving** Your school is thinking of offering an e-class: a course that you follow via the Internet with an e-mail address and video hookup so that students can "attend" their class and exchange communication with the teacher and other students while at home. A group of people wants you to make a presentation showing the benefits of this idea and listing the questions about this type of course that people may have.

To do this, follow these steps:

▶ **1.** Make a list of three possible benefits and questions. Use some of the ideas and questions from the interview to help you make this list. Work with a partner to compare your ideas.

2. Together, develop a list of three or more benefits. Prepare some examples to support your case.

3. Make a list of three questions you have about this new Internet class.

4. Share these ideas with others in a small group. Decide on a common list of benefits and questions.

5. Report on your list to the class.

▶Vocabulary Building

Word Form and Meaning

▶ **A** Match the words in Column A with their meanings in Column B.

Column A

_____ 1. confirm

_____ 2. connect

_____ 3. depress

_____ 4. recommend

_____ 5. vary

Column B

a. to change something

b. to suggest or approve of

c. to meet up with

d. to make someone unhappy

e. to make certain of

▶ **B** Study these five words in their various forms: verb, noun, adjective, and adverb. The forms are not in the same order in each column. Then choose the correct form to fill out the chart below. These words are commonly found in general and academic texts.

confirm (v.)	connect (v.)	depress (v.)	recommend (v.)	vary (v.)
confirmation (n.)	connecting	depression	recommendation	variety
confirming (adj.)	connector	depressive	recommended	variation
confirmed (adj.)	connection	depressingly	recommending	various
	connected	depressing		variously
		depressed		variable

Verb	Noun	Adjective	Adverb
connect	1.	1.	
	2.	2.	
depress	1.	1.	1.
		2.	
		3.	
recommend	1.	1.	
		2.	
vary	1.	1.	1.
	2.		
	3.		

⏵ Compare lists with a partner. Try to agree on the same answers.

⏵ **C** Write three sentences using words from the list.

Vocabulary in Context

⏵ **A** Complete each sentence with one of the words from the following list. Underline the words that helped you choose your answer.

a. concentrate   b. connect   c. notice   d. offer
e. password   f. productive   g. recommend   h. self-conscious

1. Can you _____ me to the people who produced this program so that I can ask them some questions?

2. I asked her to tell me the special _____ so that I could get into the program and get the file I needed.

3. Your work is excellent. I would be happy to _____ you for the job.

4. She was happy that they could _____ her the job she wanted.

5. I was nervous and felt very _____ about the people who were watching me.

6. I was worried and so it was difficult to _____ on finishing my work.

7. I finished all of my work after lunch. It was a very _____
   afternoon.

8. I was watching TV, so I didn't _____ how late it was.

▶ Compare your answers with a partner. Then take turns reading the completed
sentences.

▶ **B Matching Ideas and Examples** In English, writers use examples to explain a
general idea in detail. Usually, these sentences follow the statement of the idea. There
are different ways to show the reader that the writer is explaining by example. Many
writers use the words *such as, like, for example,* or *for instance* to introduce the
examples.

▶ Match the sentence in Column A with the example in Column B that fits it best.

Column A

_____ 1. My father can log on and
look at what Harry is
doing.

_____ 2. Can you see him any time
of the day?

_____ 3. I wanted to know whether
they had a good program.

_____ 4. How do you know
whether the service is
safe?

_____ 5. I lead a very busy life
most of the time.

Column B

a. I did some research to find out
whether the service has safety
precautions, for example, a special
password and a secure website.

b. For example, during the week, I
usually get up at 6:00 A.M., and I
don't stop until about 7:00 P.M.

c. For example, did they offer special
programs, such as art and reading?

d. For instance, one day, he watched
Harry writing for the first time.

e. Yes. One day, for example, I logged
on when he was in the book corner
and the teacher turned the camera
so I could see him.

▶ Compare your answers with a partner. Then take turns reading the pairs that
match.

◐ C Phrasal Verbs Write the correct preposition to complete each of the verbs in the following sentences.

1. My father can log _____ to see what his grandson is doing.

2. I wanted to show my son _____ to my boss.

3. I recommended the day-care center to my friends who were looking _____ a good school for their children.

4. I like to check _____ to see how my son is doing.

5. I decided to call _____ the company to subscribe to this service.

◐ Look at the reading to check your answers. Read the sentences with a partner.

◗Expanding Your Language

Speaking   **◐ Discussion Questions** Look at these graphs and then think about the following questions. Share your ideas with a partner or in a small group.

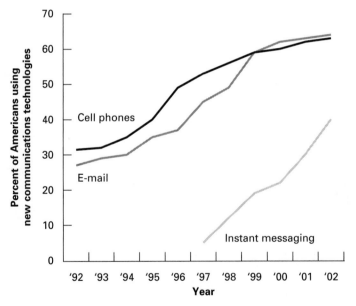

Source: Forrester Research, New York Times, *March 13, 2003*

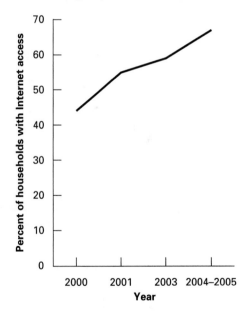

Source: U.S. Census Bureau

1. How popular is household technology becoming for Americans? What effect could this have on people?

Kids and Hi-Tech
90 percent of children 5–17 use computers
75 percent of children 14–17 use the Internet
65 percent of children 10–13 use the Internet

Teens 14–17 Report on Technology
48 percent say Internet use improves their relationships with friends
32 percent use the Internet to make new friends
74 percent use Instant Messaging

2. Why is the Internet attracting teenagers? What are the benefits and dangers?

Questionnaire   ▶ **Using the Internet** Answer these questions for yourself and add a question of your own. Ask two classmates these same questions using the chart on the next page.

Questions	You
1. Do/did you ever use the Internet?	
2. What are some useful things you can do on the Internet?	
3. What are some disadvantages to using the Internet?	
4. In the future, how will people use the Internet?	
5.	

Questions	Student A	Student B
1. Do/did you ever use the Internet?		
2. What are some useful things you can do on the Internet?		
3. What are some disadvantages to using the Internet?		
4. In the future, how will people use the Internet?		
5.		

▶ Work with a partner or in a small group. Take turns telling each other about the information you received. Share the information with others in your class.

Writing

▶ **Topic Writing** From the information in the chapter readings, discussions, and the questionnaire, make a list of three advantages and disadvantages of the Internet. Try to include one example for each of the ideas on your list.

▶ Work with a group to share the ideas on your lists. Add any ideas you can to your list. Use your list to make an outline to write from. To do this, follow the steps on page 39.

Read On: Taking It Further

Reading Cloze

Don't forget to write your in your **reading journal** and to enter new words for this chapter in your **vocabulary log**. Show your journal and log entries to your teacher. Arrange to discuss your progress in reading. ■

▶ Use the words from the unit listed here to fill in the blanks in this paragraph.

a. buy	b. communicate	c. gather	d. make	e. meet
f. rent	g. receive		h. research	i. talk	j. write

More and more people use the Internet. They (1) _____ online for many different reasons. Some people want to (2) _____ things electronically instead of going out shopping. People are using the Internet to arrange their travel. They buy tickets and (3) _____ arrangements for hotels, entertainment, and even reservations for dinner. Travelers can (4) _____ cars over the Internet. Some schools use the Internet for (5) _____. Students are able to (6) _____ information electronically. They can (7) _____ with people in faraway places. People of all ages (8) _____ other people who share their interests and (9) _____ messages to them. They send these messages by e-mail, and then they (10) _____ answers from people they have never met.

▶ Compare your answers with a partner. Try to agree on the same answers.

Newspaper Articles

▶ Every day there are new developments in technology. Ask your teacher for a short newspaper article that you can read. Choose an article about a recent development in technology discussed in this unit, such as cell phones or the Internet. Read the article over until you have a good idea of the important facts of the story. Explain your article to a partner or in a small group.

Word Play

▶ **A New-Fashioned Spelling Bee** Work in groups of four or more. Form two teams within each group. Each team makes a list of ten to fifteen (or more!) important vocabulary words in this unit. Check to make sure that you have the correct spelling. You can assign certain parts of the alphabet to avoid having words appear on both lists. Teams take turns asking the other team to spell a word on its list. The team to spell the most words correctly wins. You can make the game more difficult by varying the rules. Suggestions include using the word correctly in a sentence, spelling without writing, or spelling within a time limit.

Online Study Center   For additional activities, go to the *Reading Matters* Online Study Center at *college.hmco.com/pic/wholeyone2e.*

UNIT 6

Leisure

Time flies.

—*English Proverb*

Introducing the Topic

Leisure time is that time of the day, week, month, or year when we can do the things we enjoy or when we have time to ourselves. This unit examines the idea of leisure time in the United States today. Chapter 16 asks questions about what's happened to leisure time in today's society. How does leisure time today compare to that in the past? In Chapter 17, we compare two competing leisure activities: going out to the movies and staying home with TV or a video. Which do we prefer? Chapter 18 looks into a popular U.S. destination: the mall. What kinds of attractions do today's malls offer?

Points of Interest

What kinds of leisure activities do you think are popular today?

16 Today's Workweek: Do We Need Time Out?

Chapter Openers

Discussion Questions

▶ **Leisure Time** Think about these questions. Discuss your ideas with a partner or in a small group.

1. How much leisure time do you have
   a. every day?
   b. during the week?
   c. during the year?
2. What kinds of leisure activities do you enjoy?
3. a. How much leisure time do you think you need?
   b. Do you feel that you're getting enough time, not enough, or too much?
   c. What would you do if you had more free time?
4. Do you think that people have more leisure time today than they did 30, 50, or 100 years ago? Give reasons for your answers.

Getting Information from a Graph

▶ Look at the graph on the next page and answer these questions.

1. In what countries have the hours workers put in increased from 1990 to 2000?
2. Why do you think American workers have less leisure time than in the past?

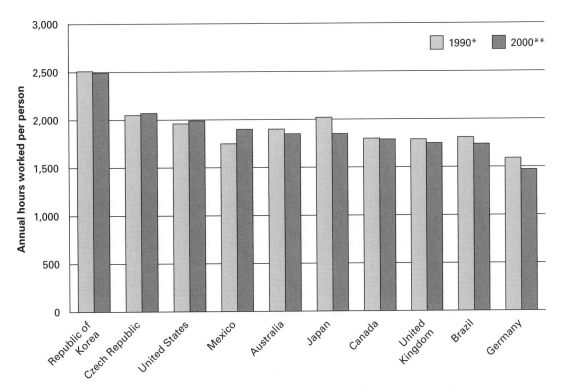

* 1991: Germany; 1991: Czech Republic
** 1998: Canada; 1999: Japan, United Kingdom, and Brazil

Exploring and Understanding Reading

Agree or Disagree?

▶ Write *A* if you agree or *D* if you disagree with the statement.

_____ 1. In the future, people will work fewer hours at their jobs.

_____ 2. People today need to work longer hours or find a second job in order to pay their bills.

_____ 3. Companies are trying to save money, so people are losing their jobs.

_____ 4. New communications technologies, such as e-mail and cell phones, give us more free time.

_____ 5. When people go on vacation, they don't bring work with them or keep in touch with their offices.

▶ Work with a partner. Compare your answers. You don't have to agree, but explain your reasons as completely as possible. After you finish reading, return to these questions and answer them based on the information you read.

Previewing

▶ To preview, read the title and the first and last sentences of each paragraph in the reading. Make a list of three ideas you expect to find out about in this reading. The first idea is done as an example.

1. Today, people are working many hours more than in the past.

2. _____

3. _____

4. _____

▶ Compare your choices with a partner. Try to agree on your answers.

▶ Read the complete article. Return to the list and change or add to your answers.

The Growth of Work

❶ In the future, people will work fewer hours a week, right? Actually, today, more people are working 10 to 12 hours a day, six days a week, than ever before in modern times. People put in the same hours as workers in the 1860–1870s did in the days before there were labor unions. In the 1950s, most people worked a 40-hour workweek. At that time, people predicted that the workweek would continue to decrease to 30 hours or less. Sociologists asked, "What will people do with all their free time?" Today, people are asking, "When will I get some free time?"

❷ More people are working longer hours, for two reasons. One reason is the increase in the cost of living. In order to support a family today, people have to work longer hours or work at a second job. Take the example of Lily P. She works in New Jersey as a social worker from 8:30 until 2:30 P.M. In the late afternoon and in the evenings, she sees private clients in her home office. On the weekends, she works as a caterer. She makes specialty cakes for weddings, anniversaries, and birthdays and delivers them to her customers. In one week, she earns about $950 to support herself and her two children. According to Lily, who is a single mother, she has to keep working the hours she does. It costs so much to support her family, she says, that working less is not possible. But there is a second reason that people are working more than 40 hours a week. Today, many companies are trying to do more work with fewer workers. These companies have reduced the number of employees in order to save money and to make higher profits. But they need to stay competitive, so they ask their employees to work longer hours.

Employees feel that they have no choice. If they don't accommodate their bosses and agree to work overtime, they are afraid that they will be fired—terminated for good.

3   Changes in technology make it easier for people to be working all the time, even when they are on vacation or with their families at home. People who work on personal computers are taking their work home with them on weekends and in the evenings. Elaine G. works for an insurance company. She works a flexible schedule so that she can be with her nine-month-old baby. She spends 24 hours a week at the office. Then she is supposed to work another 16 hours on her computer at home. She hoped that she could have more time to be with her baby. But she works more than 16 hours at home to complete her work. She says, "My boss just wants the job done. If I don't finish the work, he thinks I'm not really working at home." With faxes, cell phones, and e-mail, people can work even when they are on vacation. About thirty percent of people who answered one poll said that they checked their voice mail or answering machines once during their vacation. Some people even check their voice mail or e-mail once a day.

4   Where will technology and the demands of the workweek take us? If things continue this way into the future, we may never get to leave the office, at least not for long. Or people may begin to say, "This is enough. I need my leisure time."

Understanding Details

Reading Tip

Remember to use the **key words** of the **question** to help you look quickly and locate the answer. ▪

A Complete the statements based on the information in the reading. In the reading, underline the words that support your answers.

1. Today, people are working _____ they did in the 1860s.

2. In the 1950s, people predicted that the workweek would

_____.

3. Today, people are asking

_____.

4. In order to support a family today,

_____.

5. Today, many companies are trying to

_____.

6. People who work on personal computers are

   _____.

7. About thirty percent of people who answered one poll said

   _____.

▶ **B** Answer the following questions. In the reading, mark the question number in the margin where you found the information for your answers.

1. What are the two reasons that people are working longer hours today?

   a. _____

   b. _____

2. Why does Lily say that she has to work long hours? Which of the two reasons in question 1 relates to her situation?

   _____

3. Why does Elaine say that she has to work long hours at home? Which of the two reasons in question 1 relates to her situation?

   _____

4. With new technology, when can people work today?

   a. _____

   b. _____

5. Why does Elaine say that she has to put in more hours to finish her work at home?

   _____

6. What are two possibilities for working hours in the future?

   a. _____

   b. _____

▶ Work with a partner. Read your questions and answers. Refer to the reading if you have different answers.

Understanding Examples

In this article, we learned about the stories of two people, Lily and Elaine. They are women who are working long hours. Their experiences are examples of a general situation among many workers today.

◐ Locate the information given for these examples in the reading. In note form, write the important details of their stories.

	Lily: Supporting the Family	Elaine: Keeping the Job
Work they do		
Personal background		
Reasons for working long hours		

◐ Work with a partner. Take turns using your notes to explain these examples.

Questionnaire

◐ **Work Time/Free Time** Ask two people who are working to answer these questions. Note their answers.

Questions	Person A	Person B
1. Where do you work?		
2. What job do you do?		
3. How much time do you spend working?		
4. How much free time do you have?		
5. What do you do in your free time?		
6. In the future, would you like to have more free time? Explain your reasons.		

◐ Work with a partner or others in a small group. Report the answers to each other. Be prepared to present your results to the class.

Giving Your Opinion

▶ Based on the reading, the questionnaire reports, and your own ideas, answer the following questions.

1. Will people have more or less free time in the future? Give some reasons for your opinion.
2. How much free time would you like to have in the future?
3. What kinds of leisure activities do you think that people would like to do in the future?

▶ Discuss your ideas with a partner or in a small group.

▶Vocabulary Building

Word Form and Meaning

▶ **A** Match the words in Column A with their meanings in Column B.

Column A	Column B
_____ 1. accommodate	a. to say in advance what will happen
_____ 2. decrease	b. to end
_____ 3. demand	c. to compromise or try to please someone
_____ 4. predict	d. to have less
_____ 5. terminate	e. to ask in a forceful way

▶ **B** Study these five words in their various forms: verb, noun, adjective, and adverb. The forms are not in the same order in each column. Then choose the correct form to fill out the chart on the next page. These words are commonly found in general and academic texts.

accommodate (v.)	decrease (v.)	demand (v.)	predict (v.)	terminate (v.)
accommodation (n.)	decreased	demanding	prediction	terminally
accommodating (adj.)	decreasing	demanded	predicted	termination
accommodated (adj.)	decrease	demand	predictable	terminated
	decreasingly	demandingly	predictably	terminal
			predictor	terminator

Verb	Noun	Adjective	Adverb
decrease	1.	1. 2.	1.
demand	1.	1. 2.	1.
predict	1. 2.	1. 2.	1.
terminate	1. 2.	1. 2.	1.

▶ Compare lists with a partner. Try to agree on the same answers.

▶ **C** Write three sentences using words from the list.

Vocabulary in Context

▶ **A** Complete each sentence with one of the nouns from the list. Underline the words that helped you make your choice.

a. client   b. demands   c. employees   d. increase
e. reasons   f. schedule   g. vacation

1. She worked late so that she could meet and talk to a _____ who had an important problem to solve.

2. The company asked whether any of its _____ could stay late and work extra hours to finish the job.

3. There has been an _____ in the number of people who work a flexible schedule.

4. Everyone needs to relax and take a _____ at least once a year.

5. The workers had a list of _____ for improvement that they wanted the company to listen to.

6. I forgot my _____, so I didn't know what time I had to start work.

7. There are probably many _____ why people are working longer hours today.

B Complete each sentence with one of the verbs from the following list. Underline the words that helped you make your choice.

a. accommodate   b. check   c. complete   d. continue   e. deliver
f. hope   g. predict h. reduce   i. require   j. support

1. Can you _____ this food in time for the party tonight?

2. How long can you _____ to work without taking a break?

3. The qualifications that they _____ are what you would expect in a position of responsibility like this.

4. Would you please _____ your voice mail and see whether we've heard from that customer today?

5. They _____ the work will be finished by tomorrow night.

6. He needs enough money to be able to pay his bills and _____ himself.

7. I'd like to be able to _____ you but I can't work the hours you are asking of me.

8. Did you _____ all the work that I left for you this morning?

9. The company is in trouble, and it will have to _____ the number of workers on the night shift.

10. I don't know enough about her diet to be able to _____ what she'd like to have for dinner.

Compare your answers with a partner. Then take turns reading the sentences.

C Antonyms Match each word in Column A with its antonym in Column B.

Column A

_____ 1. fewer

_____ 2. reduce

_____ 3. answer

_____ 4. longer

_____ 5. easier

Column B

a. arrive

b. question

c. work

d. more

e. harder

_____ 6. leisure   f. impossible

_____ 7. leave   g. inflexible

_____ 8. complete   h. increase

_____ 9. possible   i. shorter

_____10. flexible   j. incomplete

▶ In English, certain prefixes, such as *il-, im-, un-, in-,* and others, are added to the beginning of an adjective to give the word its antonym, or opposite meaning.

Underline four words from the list that have an antonym that begins with one of these negative prefixes. Think of more words like these that you know.

▶Expanding Your Language

Reading

▶ **Asking Information Questions** Choose story A, which follows, or story B, which is in the "Exercise Pages" section of the book on page 251. Complete the following steps for both stories.

▶ **1.** Read the information questions about your story.

2. Read to find out the main idea of the story.

3. Underline the important facts that give the answers to the questions.

4. To compare the facts you underlined, work with a partner who read the same story.

5. Take turns asking and answering each other's questions.

6. Write the answers in note form.

7. Use your notes and take turns explaining as much of the story as you can.

Information Questions

1. What kind of vacation is this?
2. What kind of people go on this type of vacation?
3. How expensive it is?
4. What are the attractions of this kind of vacation?
5. What are the disadvantages?

A: Taking a Trip to "the Strip"

❶   In most parts of the United States, people think of Florida or California's Disney World when they think of taking a family vacation. Las Vegas is the place that people think of when they plan for some adult entertainment—such as gambling or going on their honeymoon. But Las Vegas has changed. In fact, Las Vegas is becoming a new family vacation destination. It is an exciting and attractive place to take young children. They love what this city has to offer. On one side of the main Las Vegas Boulevard is Manhattan, with a miniature Brooklyn Bridge and Statue of Liberty. Young children can visit an indoor pavilion that looks like the East Village in New York City. On the other side is Paris, with a replica of the Eiffel Tower.

❷   Each hotel has family-friendly entertainment. Treasure Island is a hotel with two large pirate ships. Every night there is a fierce battle that is staged for young guests and their parents. At the Mirage hotel there is a small zoo. There kids can see white lions and black panthers. There is even a giant dolphin tank. Next is Circus Circus—the oldest theme hotel still standing in the city. It opened in 1968. It features some old-fashioned circus treats, such as a fun house and a carousel, as well as jugglers to watch and games to play. But the circus attraction that sets Las Vegas apart for many families is the Cirque du Soleil. The Cirque offers a spectacular show that combines gymnasts with extraordinary music and theater. There are several permanent shows in Las Vegas. One show, "Mystère," attracts more than 1,400 spectators ten times a week. The water show "O" is also very popular entertainment for the whole family. Already more than five percent of all visitors to Las Vegas say that the Cirque is the main reason for coming to this tourist destination.

3   Of course, Las Vegas will always be a place to go for casinos. But it is such an entertainment paradise that you can take the kids and, after a vacation filled with action-packed days and nights, never spend a dollar on a slot machine.

Speaking

▷ **1.** Work with a partner who read story B on page 251. Explain your story to each other. Ask and answer each other's questions.

2. Use the questions and answers to help you write about one of the stories.

3. Choose a short newspaper article, like the story you read, from your local paper. Make a copy of the article and work with a partner. Follow the steps in "Asking Information Questions" on page 219 to prepare to discuss your article.

Online Study Center   For additional activities, go to the *Reading Matters* Online Study Center at *college.hmco.com/pic/wholeyone2e*.

Entertainment Choices

Chapter Openers

Categorizing

▶ Read the following statements. Write *V* if they refer to watching DVDs or videos at home, *M* if they describe going out to the movies, or *B* if they can describe both.

_____ 1. I can watch any movie I want to.

_____ 2. I can enjoy the movie with lots of other people.

_____ 3. I can see the action on a big screen.

_____ 4. I can see three movies for the price of one.

_____ 5. I can watch any time I want.

▶ Discuss your answers with a partner.

Paired Readings

▶ In this section, you will find two different stories on the same theme. Choose one of the two to work with. Prepare to explain the story to someone who read the same story and then to a person who read the other story.

▶ Each story is a personal essay written to show why the writers like the things they do. Find out the advantages and disadvantages of going out to the movies or staying home with the television.

1 At Home with the TV

Listing Reasons

▶ What are some of the reasons people stay home to watch television? List three positive reasons for spending time watching television.

1. _____

2. _____

3. _____

▶ Discuss your ideas with a partner or in a small group.

Understanding the Main Ideas

▶ Read both of the paragraphs in this reading. Write a sentence that expresses the main idea of each paragraph.

1. _____

2. _____

Understanding Details

▶ Answer the questions after each paragraph. Underline the facts in the reading that support your answer. Write the question number in the margin of the reading.

Confessions of a Couch Potato

❶   I have a confession to make. My idea of a perfect evening is to stay at home, eat in, and watch TV. There are so many good shows on these days. And there are so many new channels. I could watch television all night. There's broadcasting 24 hours a day. First, I'll catch the news. With cable, I get two 24-hour news stations. There's even a station that shows the news every 15 minutes. Some nights, I'll watch a news documentary. There's a documentary shown every night of the week on at least one channel. Then there're the sit-coms.  The funny ones are on early in the evening. The dramatic shows are on later. After that there's the late-night news and, of course, late-night talk shows. Of course, that only represents what's on during the week. On the weekends, I don't watch TV; well, not exactly.

1. What is the author's idea of a perfect evening?

_____

2. How many hours of broadcasting can this person watch?

_____

3. How many 24-hour news stations does this person get?

_____

4. How often does one station show the news?

_____

5. What are three other kinds of programs this person likes to watch?

a. _____

b. _____

c. _____

6. Does this person watch TV on the weekend?

_____

❷   On the weekends, I go to my video store and get a few good movies to watch on my DVD player or VCR. I would rather watch a movie at home than go out. It costs less and I can really get comfortable. I can pause the movie when I want to get up and get something to eat. I'm not exactly a couch potato. That's because I don't watch television in the living room, where my couch is. My television is in my bedroom. So I can watch while I'm in bed. I know it's not a good habit, but insomnia is not something I worry about. Maybe I should worry about watching so much TV and not getting out enough.

1. What does the author do on the weekends?

_____

2. Why would the author rather watch a movie at home?

_____

3. Why isn't this person a couch potato?

_____

4. Where does the author watch TV?

_____

5. a. What does the author not worry about?

   _____

   b. What should the author worry about?

   _____

▶ Work with a partner. Take turns reading the questions and answers. Refer to the information in the reading if you have different answers.

Recapping the Information

▶ Work with a partner who read the same story. Together, underline the important facts in both paragraphs. Then use the information to complete a note-taking outline like this one:

The Perfect Night In
- stay at home
- eat in
- watch TV
Programs I Like to Watch
   …

▶ Practice telling the information to your partner. Try not to read the notes as you speak. Ask for help if you forget or give incorrect information.

Reacting to the Information

▶ Make a list of three or four reasons for and against staying home to watch TV. Use information from the reading and ideas of your own. Write your ideas in note form, as shown in the following chart.

Advantages	Disadvantages
1. Being comfortable at home	Not getting physical exercise
2.	
3.	
4.	

▶ Work with a partner and share your ideas. Together, make a list of your best ideas to share with others.

▶ Discuss this question with others: Is staying home to watch television a good idea? Why or why not?

❷Out at the Movies

Listing Reasons

▷ What are some of the reasons people like to go out to the movies? List three positive reasons for choosing to see a movie in a theater.

1. _____

2. _____

3. _____

▷ Discuss your ideas with a partner or in a small group.

Understanding the Main Ideas

▷ Read both of the paragraphs that follow. Write a sentence that expresses the main idea of each paragraph.

1. _____

2. _____

Understanding Details

▷ Answer the questions after each paragraph. Underline the facts in the reading that support your answer. Write the question number in the margin of the reading.

Confessions of a Movie Fan

❶   On a cold winter night, I know that there are lots of reasons to stay home and watch DVDs or videos, but I love to go out to the movies. The films look better in the theater. The screen is so wide that it seems to surround you. You really get the feeling that you are closer to the action. The costumes and the settings look so much more beautiful on the big screen. And, of course, because of the equipment and the acoustics in the theater, the sound is so much better, too. The special effects don't look or sound as good at home. Plus, I like seeing a movie with other people in the theater. The reaction of the crowd can intensify my feelings. I like noticing the parts of the movie that people laugh at or cry over. I like listening to the reaction of people after the movie is over. I even like watching the previews and the special messages before the movie starts. The previews can be really funny, and they help me to decide whether I want to see the film when it comes out. Last, but not least, I love the popcorn.

1. What does the author love to do?

   _____

2. Why is the sound better at the movies?

   _____

3. How does seeing special effects at the movies compare to seeing them at home?

   _____

4. Why does the author like seeing movies with other people in the theater?

   _____

5. Why does the author like the previews?

   _____

❷ Seeing a movie is a social event. I enjoy going out and making an evening of it. If I'm with a friend, we'll go and have coffee either before or after the film. It's really my idea of a good date. If there's a film I especially like, I'll invite someone out and see it again. If the film is very moving or extremely well done, I might go back two or three times. If I'm alone, I usually go during the week when the ticket price is lower. On the weekend, the tickets are more expensive and the lines are very long. I like going with friends to repertoire theaters. You can see some of the old classics or movies by a well-known director. The theater gives a special student rate, so we don't have to pay much to go. In some cities, there are film festivals that show new and experimental films. At the festival, there are a lot of people who come to see these films. There is often a lot of excitement at these events.

1. What does the author enjoy doing?

   _____

2. Where does the author like to go before or after a film?

   _____

3. How many times does the author like to go to see a movie?

   _____

4. Why is it better to go to a film during the week?

   _____

5. What other kinds of films does the author like to see?

   _____

▶ Work with a partner. Take turns reading the questions and answers. Refer to the information in the reading if you have different answers.

Recapping the Information

▶ Work with a partner who read the same information. Together, underline the important facts in both paragraphs. Then use the information to complete a note-taking outline like this one:

The Perfect Night Out
• go to the movies—even if it's cold
Reasons I Prefer Movies
• films look better on wide screen; feel you are there
• beautiful costumes
   …

▶ Practice telling the information to your partner. Try not to read the notes as you speak. Ask for help if you forget or give incorrect information.

Reacting to the Information

▶ Make a list of three or four reasons for and against going out to the movies. Use information from the reading and ideas of your own. Write your ideas in note form, as shown in the following chart.

Advantages	Disadvantages
1. Enjoyment of seeing images on the large screen	Waiting in long lines
2.	
3.	
4.	

▶ Work with a partner and share your ideas. Together, make a list of your best ideas to share with others.

▶ Discuss this question with others: What are the reasons why you like going out to the movies?

Comparing the Readings

Discussing the Stories

▶ Work with a partner who read a different story. Use your notes, charts, and discussion questions to explain the information.

▶ Discuss the following question: What makes watching TV at home or going out to the movies fun for you?

❶Vocabulary Building

Word Form and Meaning

❷ **A** Match the words in Column A with their meanings in Column B.

Column A

_____ 1. effect

_____ 2. invite

_____ 3. pause

_____ 4. surround

_____ 5. represent

Column B

a. to stand for something

b. to stop for a moment

c. to completely encircle

d. to ask someone to visit

e. to cause to occur

❷ **B** Study these five words in their various forms: verb, noun, adjective, and adverb. The forms are not in the same order in each column. Then choose the correct form to fill out the chart below. These words are commonly found in general and academic texts.

effect (v.)	invite (v.)	pause (v.)	represent (v.)	surround (v.)
effect (n.)	invitee	paused	representation	surroundings
effected (adj.)	invitingly	pausing	represented	surrounding
effective (adj.)	invited	pause	representative	surrounded
effecting (adj.)	inviting		representatively	
effectively (adv.)	invitation			

Verb	Noun	Adjective	Adverb
invite	1.	1.	1.
	2.	2.	
pause	1.	1.	
		2.	
represent	1.	1.	1.
		2.	
surround	1.	1.	
		2.	

❷ Compare lists with a partner. Try to agree on the same answers.

▶ **C** Write three sentences using words from the list.

Vocabulary in Context

▶ **A Antonyms** Match each word in Column A with its antonym in Column B.

Column A	Column B
_____ 1. overlooked	a. arrived
_____ 2. laugh	b. narrow
_____ 3. special	c. slowly
_____ 4. get up	d. appreciated
_____ 5. quickly	e. never
_____ 6. left	f. ordinary
_____ 7. always	g. finish
_____ 8. start	h. cry
_____ 9. wide	i. sit down

▶ Compare your answers with a partner. Write three or more sentences, using at least two of the words from the lists in each sentence.

▶ **B Categorizing** Circle the word or phrase that does not belong in each of these groups. Tell why it doesn't belong there.

1. 24 hours   station   evening   late night   weekend
2. dramatic   documentary   sit-coms   news programs   channels
3. costumes   settings   acoustics   special effects   previews
4. video store   bed   living room   couch   bedroom
5. usually   quickly   interesting   really   very

Expanding Your Language

Reading

Some people like to find a hobby to pursue in their leisure time. Read about one man's unusual hobby and find out why it is such an important leisure activity. Think about hobbies that you might enjoy. Notice how much easier it is to understand this story now that you have already done some reading on the topic of leisure.

▶ Before beginning, read the following questions. After reading, answer them based on the information in the text.

1. What is vexillology?
2. What has Cannon pursued his whole life?
3. When did he begin this hobby? How long has he followed it?
4. What is in his collection?
5. Where has he donated his flags?
6. What other activities has he carried out?
7. Why is he interested in this hobby?

A Hobby for Life

There is one man who knows the meaning of the word vexillology. Colonel D. Cannon knows that it means the study of flags. He knows it because collecting flags is a hobby that he has pursued his whole life. At the young age of four, Cannon began studying flags, drawing them in his coloring books and putting them up on his walls. Throughout school, he studied flags and tried to find out all he could about them. After university, Cannon studied to be a lawyer. Throughout law school, he continued to collect flags. His classmates, friends, and family started calling him "the flagman."

Cannon now has more than 200 flags in his collection. He displays many of them in his downtown law office. He lends them to schools and community organizations when they need them. For example, he donated his flags to the local high school for a display of African flags during Black History Month. And he donated country flags for an exhibit on the Olympics.

In addition to collecting flags, Cannon also writes about them. He has published three books about flags. He loves to hear from friends who see his books in stores all over the world. A few years ago, Cannon's hobby reached a new level. He entered a flag design contest and won. The county he lives in asked him to design its flag. He used his mother's sewing machine and made the flag in his evenings and on weekends. Cannon explains his hobby this way, "Collecting flags is like collecting pieces of history."

Speaking

▶ **Movie Review** Work with a partner or in a small group. Choose a movie that everyone in the group can agree they would like to see together. Together, prepare to talk about the important elements of the movie you will see. Prepare to answer the following questions about the movie.

1. What is the name of the movie?
2. What kind of movie is it?
   - comedy
   - romance
   - action
   - drama
   - science fiction
   - biography
   - history
3. Who are the main characters?
4. What are the main parts of the story, or plot, of the film?
5. Where and when does the movie take place?
6. Would you tell other people to see this movie? Why or why not?

▶ **A** After the movie, get together with others and answer the questions above. Takes notes of the answers. Practice explaining about the movie to each other.

▶ **B** Get together with a partner who saw a different movie and talk about the movie you saw.

Writing

▶ Use the notes you prepared for your movie review to write about the movie you saw.

🔆 *Online Study Center*   For additional activities, go to the *Reading Matters* Online Study Center at *college.hmco.com/pic/wholeyone2e*.

18 Meeting at the Mall: America's Growing Leisure Activity

◖Chapter Openers

Discussion Questions

▶ Think about these questions. Share your ideas with a partner or in a small group.

1. Why are shopping malls popular?
2. *Compare:* How are shopping malls in other countries similar to or different from those in the United States?

Matching

▶ Match each of these activities to the correct illustration. Check (✔) the activities that you think people go to malls to do. Think of as much information as possible to explain your choices.

a.   b.   c.   d.

e.   f.   g.   h.

_____ 1. jogging

_____ 2. meeting friends to talk

_____ 3. window shopping

_____ 4. going to a movie

_____ 5. sightseeing

_____ 6. riding a roller coaster

_____ 7. playing in a video arcade

_____ 8. meeting other teens

Exploring and Understanding Reading

Previewing

▷ In English, writers often state the main idea in the first one or two sentences of the paragraph. Read the beginning sentences of each paragraph of the reading. Write the number of the paragraph that best fits each of these main idea statements.

_____ a. The interest tourists have in visiting the largest malls in the United States

_____ b. The many activities local people can do at the mall

_____ c. The increasing interest in visiting malls in the United States

_____ d. The good and bad effects of malls on the economy

◗ Compare your answers with a partner. Read the whole article and confirm your answers.

It's a Mall World After All

❶   What is the favorite destination in the United Sates? It's not a national park or the Statue of Liberty. It's the mall. Malls are attracting

more and more people. Malls were designed for people to get all of their shopping done conveniently. Malls used to be called "shopping centers." But today, people who are heading for the malls have more than shopping in mind. In fact, for some people, shopping is the last thing they're thinking of.

❷   There are more than 300 malls in the United States, and the largest contain more than 200 different shops. The Mall of America in Bloomington, Minnesota, is one of the country's largest malls. It has more than 400 stores, 50 restaurants, 9 nightclubs, and a roller coaster. In 1995, about 40 million people visited this huge shopping center. Some of the visitors were tourists. People visiting from overseas want to buy presents to bring home to families and friends. But that is not the only reason they come. Some tourists want to experience what they describe as "consumer heaven." One young man from France expressed his feelings this way, "Now that we've seen the sights at the mall, we can go home." Some people plan their vacations around their shopping plans. Some malls are planning big entertainment centers to add to their appeal. In Washington, more people visit the Potomac Mills shopping center than visit Mount Vernon or Arlington National Cemetery. Potomac Mills attracts about 660,000 international shoppers and 23 million domestic shoppers each year.

❸   Large malls attract tourists, but the small malls in cities and towns throughout the country are attractive to locals, especially teens and seniors. Why do these people come to the mall? Malls are becoming popular spots for older people to get together for their morning exercise. Jack Donner and his wife, Margo, meet up at 7:00 A.M. with six friends in their seventies for a eight-mile daily hike. They wear running shoes and jogging outfits and walk at a fast pace through the mall. By 10:00 they are ready for a break and breakfast at their favorite café, which is in the mall. According to Jack, the mall suits their needs perfectly. It's a safe place, it's protected from the weather, it's quiet, and, at 7:00 A.M., not crowded. Shopping is secondary; the mall's a good place to socialize. Socializing is also on the minds of teenagers, who come to the malls after school and on the weekends. Kids meet their friends to talk. They walk around and look at what's on sale, but they don't spend a lot of money on shopping. They spend most of the afternoon sitting on the benches outside the food courts, just hanging out with their friends.

❹   Some people say that malls are good for the economy. They provide jobs and taxes for the government. But others criticize the traffic jams, the crowds, and the low-paying jobs that are available to most of the people who work there. Environmentalists complain that the builders and developers are destroying good farm and forest land when they put up these large malls. Some people say that malls take business away from small stores and local family businesses. Some parents say that they don't like their kids to spend their free time sitting around talking and looking at things to buy. But others like the convenience of malls, and they like paying lower prices at the big discount stores found there. Malls may not appeal to everyone, but throughout the United States, they are a favorite destination for many.

Understanding Details

▶ In note form, write the answers to the questions. In the reading, underline the words that support your answers. Write the question number in the margin.

1. What is America's favorite destination?

   _____

2. a. How many malls are there in the United States?

   _____

   b. What do the largest contain?

   _____

3. List these important details about the Mall of America:

   a. Location: _____

   b. Number of stores: _____

   c. Number of restaurants: _____

   d. Number of nightclubs: _____

   e. Visitors: _____

4. What are two reasons that tourists visit the mall?

   a. _____

   b. _____

5. What three details show that U.S. malls are popular with tourists?

   a. _____

   b. _____

   c. _____

6. What two groups of people like visiting malls near their homes?

   a. _____

   b. _____

   ▶ Work with a partner. Read your questions and answers. Refer to the reading if you have different answers.

Identifying the Facts

▶ Identify facts from the reading below, then work with a partner and take turns explaining your answers.

1. List these important details about activities in the malls:

	Older People	Teenagers
Activity:	_____	_____
When:	_____	_____
How long:	_____	_____
Advantages:	_____	_____

2. What do people say about the effect of malls on the economy?

   a. Positive effects: _____

   b. Negative effects: _____

Identifying the Speaker

▶ **Who Said That?** Read and identify the speaker for each of the statements, based on the information in the reading. Write *T* for tourist, *S* for senior, and *TE* for teenager.

_____ 1. One of the things I most wanted to do while I was here was to visit this mall. I just couldn't go home without getting presents for people back home.

_____ 2. She told me that she'd meet me here right after school. It's almost five o'clock. I'm going to have to get home soon, but I've got to talk to her.

_____ 3. Come with me and look at this dress. I don't have enough for it, but it would look great on you.

_____ 4. Come and join us tomorrow morning. Wear something comfortable, and meet us in front of Little Jack's at 7:00.

_____ 5. The guard told us we had to leave. We can't sit in the food court after 11:30 P.M.

_____ 6. This is the most amazing place. I saw it advertised at the travel bureau, but I really couldn't imagine how big and crowded it would be. There's so much here; I could spend the whole day walking around.

_____ 7. Judy told me that there's this really good-looking boy who is always here with his friends.

▶ Work with a partner. Take turns reading and then identifying whose statements these could be.

Evaluating the Information

▶ **Reading from the News** Read the short article that follows, and then discuss these questions.

1. What are some churches doing?
2. Why are they doing this?
3. Where is the Anglican Church located?
4. What are some of the feelings, both positive and negative, that people have about this new church location?

Churches in Malls Give New Meaning to Sunday Shopping

Some churches are now holding services in retail malls as an added attraction to one-stop Sunday shopping. The move is aimed at bringing new members to churches that are in financial trouble. According to Paul MacLean, a consultant for the Anglican Church of Canada, "Malls are the great collecting points of people in our culture now." The church is out in the marketplace, along with clothing stores, fast-food joints, and all of that. According to the Anglican Church, it has been a mixed success. Malls are attracting a lot of people. There's a lot of energy. But there's a problem. It doesn't feel like a church to some people.

What's your opinion? Are malls a good location for religious services?

❶Vocabulary Building

Word Form and Meaning

▶ **A** Match the words in Column A with their meanings in Column B.

Column A	Column B
_____ 1. complain	a. to feel or live through something
_____ 2. consume	b. to ruin
_____ 3. destroy	c. to build
_____ 4. develop	d. to use up
_____ 5. experience	e. to express unhappiness

▶ **B** Study these five words in their various forms: verb, noun, adjective, and adverb. The forms are not in the same order in each column. Then choose the correct form to fill out the chart below. These words are commonly found in general and academic texts.

complain (v.)	consume (v.)	destroy (v.)	develop (v.)	experience (v.)
complaint (n.)	consumed	destroying	developing	experience
complainer (n.)	consumption	destruction	development	experientially
complaining (adj.)	consuming	destroyed	developed	experienced
complainingly (adv.)	consumer	destroyer	developer	experiential
		destructively		

Verb	Noun	Adjective	Adverb
consume	1. 2.	1. 2.	
destroy	1. 2.	1. 2.	1.
develop	1. 2.	1. 2.	
experience	1.	1. 2.	1.

▶ Compare lists with a partner. Try to agree on the same answers.

▶ **C** Write three sentences using words from the list.

▶ **D** Decide whether the word in boldface is a noun (*N*) or a verb (*V*). Then write five sentences of your own, showing how to use five of the words in boldface as a different part of speech.

_____ 1. We decided to go to the gym and **exercise** after work.

_____ 2. A nice long **walk** will be good for you.

_____ 3. I think the **pace** of life today is too slow.

_____ 4. I liked the **design** of the old building better than the new.

_____ 5. Visiting the old city was the best **experience** of the trip.

_____ 6. She decided to organize the **visit** for a time when we could be together.

_____ 7. They got together to **plan** the surprise birthday party.

▶ Compare your answers with a partner. Then take turns reading the sentences.

Vocabulary in Context

▶ Use a word from the following list to complete the sentences. Underline the words that helped you to choose your answers.

a. attract	b. contain	c. criticize	d. describe	e. experience
f. express	g. meet	h. provide	i. socialize	j. spend

1. They want to _____ how it feels to live in another country.

2. They often _____ their friends at the mall for coffee and conversation.

3. The new store will _____ jobs for many people in the area.

4. I have no more money to _____ on new clothes this month.

5. I found three birthday cards with messages that _____ my feelings exactly.

6. They put up beautiful new signs to _____ customers to their stores.

7. Can you _____ what the new shopping center looks like?

8. I don't like to _____ but this food tastes terrible.

9. These boxes _____ all the parts you'll need to finish the project.

10. This place is so popular that everyone goes there to _____ .

▶ Compare your answers with a partner. Then take turns reading the sentences.

Expanding Your Language

Speaking

▶ You read that malls are a tourist attraction in the United States. What is your idea of a good place to visit when you are on vacation?

▶ Look at the following graphs. Based on the information in the graphs, answer the following questions. Work with a partner or a small group to discuss your answers.

1. What activity do most people plan **after** they arrive at their destination?

   _____

2. What activities attract the same percentage of people?

   _____

3. a. What activities are less popular than others?

   _____

   b. What activities are more popular than others?

   _____

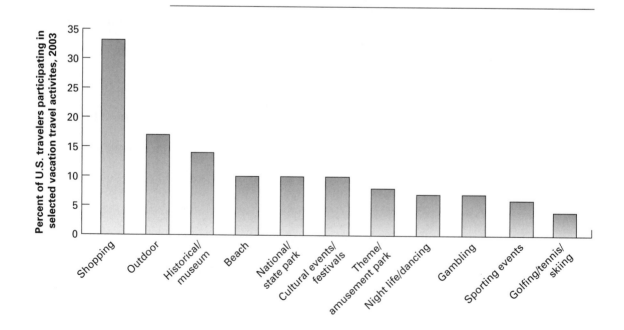

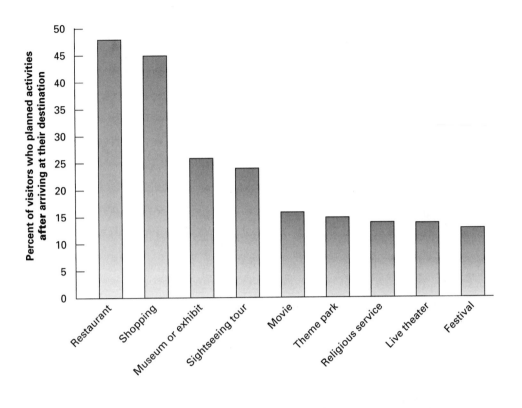

▶ **Questionnaire** Answer these questions for yourself. Ask two others the same questions using the chart on the next page.

Questions	You
1. Where would you like to go on vacation?	

2. What would you like to do on vacation?
  • read
  • play sports
  • travel
  • visit friends and family
  • go shopping	

3. How often would you like to take a vacation?	
4. How long would you like to spend on vacation?	

5. Who would you like to go on vacation with?
  • family member
  • friend
  • alone	

Questions	Student A	Student B
1. Where would you like to go on vacation?		
2. What would you like to do on vacation? • read • play sports • travel • visit friends and family • go shopping		
3. How often would you like to take a vacation?		
4. How long would you like to spend on vacation?		
5. Who would you like to go on vacation with? • family member • friend • alone		

▶ Work with a partner. Take turns explaining the information you gathered. Share your information with others in the class.

Writing

▶ **Topic Writing** Write a paragraph about the advantages and disadvantages of malls. Write some sentences about the advantages and others about the disadvantages. Use the information you read about in this chapter and any ideas of your own.

To carry out this task, follow these steps:

▶ **1.** Reread the articles in this chapter and brainstorm a list of good and bad points about malls. Discuss these ideas with others in a small group. Try to add ideas to your list.

2. Make an outline of the information you plan to include. Refer to Chapter 3, page 39, for an example of how to outline.

3. Work with a partner. Use your outline to explain what you plan to write. Make any changes necessary to complete your outline.

4. Write the paragraph.

5. Work with a partner and explain to each other the ideas you wrote about.

6. Give the paragraph to your teacher.

Read On: Taking It Further

Reading Cloze

> **Reading Tip**

Look over your **reading journal** and **vocabulary log** entries. Look over the reading work you have done in this book. Prepare to discuss this question: How has my reading improved? ■

Use the words from the unit listed here to fill in the blanks in this paragraph.

| a. arrange | b. carry | c. check | d. forget | e. keep |
| f. never | g. possible | h. provide | i. travel | j. work |

Usually, American workers get two weeks of vacation a year. But today, more Americans are taking (1) _____ with them when they go on vacation. With today's technology, a person can (2) _____ to another country and still (3) _____ in touch with the home office. With cell phones and e-mail, the office is (4) _____ far away. Many people (5) _____ their e-mail during their vacation. People (6) _____ their cell phones on the beach. Many tour companies (7) _____ to have Internet access for their clients on cruise ships. Hotels (8) _____ computers for their guests. Some people say that this technology makes it (9) _____ to go on vacation. Other people say that when they go on vacation, they want to be able to (10) _____ about work.

Compare your answers with a partner. Try to agree on the same answers.

Newspaper Articles

▶ Check the newspaper for articles about leisure and leisure activities like those you read about in this unit. Ask your teacher for short articles that you can read. One suggestion is to look for articles about places to visit and things to do that you can find in the travel or entertainment sections of the newspaper. Read the article over until you have a good idea of the important facts of the story. Explain your article to a partner or in a small group.

Word Play

▶ Choose one of the word-play activities described in the "Read On" sections of Unit 2 (page 79), Unit 4 (page 161), and Unit 5 (page 207). Carry out the activity you chose with others in a small group.

 **Online Study Center**   For additional activities, go to the *Reading Matters* Online Study Center at *college.hmco.com/pic/wholeyone2e*.

Exercise Pages

UNIT 1 **Communication: Talking to €ach Other**

Chapter ❸ Leave Me a Message

Categorizing

▶ **B** Read the messages and decide which category each best belongs in. Write *W* for work, *S* for school, and *H* for home. Some messages might fit in more than one category.

Set B

1. _____ The paper is due next Thursday.

2. _____ We're out of milk. Pick up a few quarts.

3. _____ Judy wants you to meet her at the library to study for the final.

4. _____ Let's meet for lunch near my office and talk about the project.

▶ **C** Compare your answers with a partner. Try to agree on the same answers.

▶ **D** Work with a partner who chose the messages in Set A. Take turns reading to each other the messages in both Set A and Set B. Decide which categories your partner's messages belong in.

▶ **E** Now turn to page 30 and complete Part E of the activity.

UNIT 5   **Technology for Today's World**

Chapter ⓭ Food for the Twenty-First Century

Reading

▷ **Asking Information Questions** Student B: Work with the story that follows. (Student A works with the story on page 174.) Complete the following steps.

▷ **1.** Read the information questions about your story.

2. Read the story to find the main idea.

3. Underline the important facts that give the answers to the questions.

4. Work with a partner who read the same story to compare the facts you underlined.

5. Take turns asking and answering each other's questions.

6. Write your answers in note form.

7. Use your notes and take turns explaining as much of the story as you can.

Information Questions

1. Who developed this technology?
2. What is it used for?
3. How does it work?
4. What are the benefits?
5. Where is it used?

B: A Solar Cooker

The solar cooker is a great invention for sunny countries in which there are not many trees. It is a simple combination of aluminum foil inside a cardboard box that opens up to reflect the sun's rays and create heat. A dark-colored pot is placed inside the open box. The heat from the sun hits the foil and is transferred to the pot. The solar cooker can be used to boil water and to prepare food. This simple system was developed by workers of a company that advises rural citizens in African countries. The benefit to the people is that it saves the time it would take to find wood and the money that could be used to buy more food instead of wood or other kinds of fuel.

Speaking

1. Work with a partner who read story A on page 174. Explain your story to each other. Use the illustration to help you explain. Ask and answer each other's questions.

2. Together, make a list of the similarities and differences between your two stories.

3. Share your ideas with your classmates.

4. Use the questions and answers to help you write about each of the stories.

UNIT 6 **Leisure**

Chapter ⑯ Today's Workweek: Do We Need Time Out?

Reading

Asking Information Questions Student B: Work with the story that follows. (Student A works with the story on page 220.) Complete the following steps.

▷ **1.** Read the information questions about your story.
  2. Read to find out the main idea of the story.
  3. Underline the important facts that give the answers to the questions.
  4. Work with a partner who read the same story to compare the facts you underlined.
  5. Take turns asking and answering each other's questions.
  6. Write the answers in note form.
  7. Use your notes and take turns explaining as much of the story as you can.

Information Questions

1. What kind of vacation is this?
2. What kind of people go on this type of vacation?
3. How expensive it is?
4. What are the attractions of this kind of vacation?
5. What are the disadvantages?

B: Destination Solitude at the Nada Monastery

❶   Many vacationers like to go to popular resorts where there are lots of people and activities. But not everyone likes this kind of vacation. The Nada Monastery is one example of the kind of vacation destination that is attracting people who are looking for some peace and quiet. The Nada Monastery is a retreat in the mountains of Colorado in the western United States. People who come to the monastery pay US $300 a week for a cabin that is set back in the trees up in the hills. There people can eat simple vegetarian food, go for hikes on mountain trails, or just sit and read or enjoy the view. The retreat is far from civilization; the closest town is fifty miles away. The retreat is hidden away up in the mountains.

❷   The Nada Monastery is a good place to come to relax and regain energy. The monks who live there find that all of their guests can benefit from an opportunity to get away from today's rushed, materialistic world. They offer people a simple lifestyle. They feel the monastery gives people the chance to reconnect to their true selves. Guests to the monastery do not have any schedule that they must follow. They can spend their days writing, reading, meditating, or praying as they please. The monks themselves make sure that their days include time for leisure. They say that leisure is as important as work because it helps them to keep a proper balance in their lives. The monks have come from different walks of life. One of them was a successful medical researcher before coming to the monastery. She believes that play is an important part of life. At the monastery she says she laughs a lot. Living in this wilderness area brings her a joy that she appreciates every day.

❸   The monks have established four monasteries over the past forty years. But only two remain—the wilderness monastery in Colorado and one in Ireland. The other two, in Arizona and in Canada, were abandoned when developers came too close and disturbed the quiet that the monks feel is so special about their retreat.

Speaking

▶ 1. Work with a partner who read story A. Explain your story to each other. Ask and answer each other's questions.

2. Use the questions and answers to help you write about one of the stories.

3. Choose a short newspaper article, like the story you read, from your local paper. Make a copy of the article and work with a partner. Follow the steps in "Asking Information Questions" on page 219 to prepare to discuss your article.